S. S. R.

$12

Amur R.

Nikolayevsk

Komsomolsk

Khabarovsk

KURIL IS.

Tsitsihar

MARITIME PROV.

SHIKOTAN I.
HABOMAI IS.

Harbin

HOKKAIDO

Liao R.

Changchun

Sapporo

GARI

Mukden

Vladivostok

Hakodate

Port Authur

P'yongyang

Niigata

Sendai

Tientsin

Dairen

Seoul

KOREA

HONSHU

Tsinan

Tokyo

Tsingtao

Pusan

Nagoya

J A P A N

Hsuchow

Hiroshima

Kobe

Kyoto

Yokohama

uai R.

TSU IS.

Shimonoseki

Osaka

Nanking

Nagasaki

SHIKOKU

J A P A N

nkow
(Wuhan)

Shanghai

KYUSHU

Hangchow

Ningpo

PACIFIC OCEAN

Nanchang

AMAMI IS.

OKINAWA

Foochow

BONIN IS.

watow

Taipei

RYUKYU IS.

IWO I.

Amoy

PESCADORES

TAIWAN

NG
NG

EAST ASIA

A BRIEF
DIPLOMATIC HISTORY
OF MODERN JAPAN

A BRIEF
DIPLOMATIC

HISTORY OF MODERN JAPAN

by Morinosuke Kajima

CHARLES E. TUTTLE CO.: PUBLISHERS
Rutland, Vermont & Tokyo, Japan

Representatives

For Continental Europe:
BOXERBOOKS, INC., Zurich

For the British Isles:
PRENTICE-HALL INTERNATIONAL, INC., London

For Australasia:
PAUL FLESCH & CO., PTY. LTD., Melbourne

Published by the Charles E. Tuttle Company, Inc.
of Rutland, Vermont and Tokyo, Japan
with editorial offices at
Suido 1-chome, 2–6, Bunkyo-ku, Tokyo

Library of Congress Catalog Card No. 65–22112

First edition, 1965
Second printing, 1966

Book design and typography by Keiko Chiba
Title page ink painting by Ume Kajima
Printed in Japan

Contents

Preface

THE MAIN purpose in publishing the English version of my original book entitled *Nippon Gaiko no Tembo* is to present to foreign readers a brief historical background of Japan's diplomacy.

In view of the growing importance of Japan in world affairs, particularly in Asia, a better understanding of the past and present circumstances which have influenced the course of her policy is exceedingly important.

I delivered a lecture at the Japan Maritime Club on the subject of "Japan's Past, Present and Future Foreign Policy" on November 25, 1963, in compliance with the request of the Association for Disseminating Knowledge on Diplomatic Affairs. The transcribed copies of this lecture, published in Pamphlet No. 43 of the Association, were distributed to the members.

It was shortly thereafter that I was informed by the Jiji Press Ltd. that they were interested in publishing a book based on the pamphlet, but supplemented by more detailed clarifications. Since my special subject of study is Japan's diplomatic history from the early years of Meiji up to World War II, I had not only read most of the significant official documents in the Foreign Ministry archives, but had also published several books related to Japan's foreign policy, such as *A Diplomatic History of Japan and Great Britain, Diplomatic History of Japan and the United States,* and the *Historical Study of Japan's Foreign Policy.* In addition, as a supplement to the foregoing books, I wrote the *Study of the Causes of World War I.*

In view of these circumstances, my lecture was primarily focused on Japan's past diplomatic policy, with only a cursory reference to the present and future foreign policy.

In publishing the Japanese edition of the book entitled *Nippon Gaiko no Tembo,* stress was laid on the present and future of Japan's diplomatic policy, limiting the account of the past, as contained in the original lecture, only to further details and explanations.

The essential aim of this book is to review the development of Japan's foreign policy, beginning from the postwar recovery of national sovereignty up to the present time, stressing at the same time some of the major pending diplomatic issues.

Just as the course of Japan's past foreign policy was governed by the shifts in Anglo-Japanese relations and the related questions between Japan and China, so the present and future course of this nation's foreign policy will be largely determined by the developments in the relations between Japan, on the one hand, and the United States and China, on the other.

I shall, of course, be highly gratified if this book serves to promote a clearer understanding of Japan's diplomatic history.

I should like to express my sincere gratitude to Mr. Yuichiro Isobe, staff member of the Kajima Institute of Research, to whom I entrusted the translation of *Nippon Gaiko no Tembo,* and to Mr. Seiichiro Katsurayama for his counsel

and assistance. Last, but not least, I am grateful to Mr.
Charles E. Tuttle for having undertaken the publication of
this book in the English language.

Tokyo   *Morinosuke Kajima*

NOTE: All Japanese names that appear in the text are given according to the Japanese custom, the family name first followed by their given name.

A BRIEF
DIPLOMATIC HISTORY
OF MODERN JAPAN

CHAPTER 1

Opening Japan to Foreign Intercourse

T
HE CURTAIN rises on the modern diplomatic history of Japan with the opening of the country to foreign intercourse by the Tokugawa Shogunate. While the visit to Uraga in July, 1853, of four American "black ships" under Commodore Perry ignited the fuse leading to the opening of our country, national sentiments were gravely disturbed by the appearance at Nagasaki in August of four Russian warships commanded by Admiral Poutiatine.

However, even decades earlier, the unwelcome vanguards of Western powers had already been extending their tentacles towards Japan, not a few of them without territorial designs over the island nation.

As a consequence of the Opium War with China, Great Britain, striking out from her base of operations in India, succeeded in gaining a firm foothold on the Chinese mainland, taking possession of Hong Kong in 1842.

In order to forestall a similar British incursion into Japan, Commodore Perry, prior to paying his momentous visit to Japan, had recommended to President Millard Fillmore the advisability of taking possession of Ryukyu Islands or Bonin Islands, as a base for the U.S. exploitation of Japan.

13

A few decades earlier, the Russians, driving eastward across Siberia and southward to the Kuril Islands and Sakhalin, began to appear in ships off Soya in Hokkaido and Etorofu Island (Staten Island). A Russian mission appeared first at Nemuro, then at Nagasaki, requesting trade and diplomatic relations between the two countries, but on both occasions the Shogunate adamantly refused either to alter its traditional policy or to accept the Tsar's gifts.

It was at this critical juncture that the hard-pressed Shogunate began to pay serious attention to coastal defense, with particular regard to its administration of Hokkaido. It instructed Mogami Tokunai, Kondo Shigezo, and Mamiya Rinzo, three of Japan's foremost explorers, to explore and survey the Kuril Islands and Sakhalin. The cry of *"jo-i,"* or "expel the foreigners," gathered new momentum as outrages by Russians against the Shogunate's northernmost garrisons mounted in the Kurils and Sakhalin, and British warships boldly intruded into Nagasaki harbor. Finally, in April, 1825, the Shogunate proclaimed its famous decree for the expulsion of all foreign vessels *(ikokusen uchi harai rei),* by which Japan tried to strictly adhere to its national policy of seclusion.

But the visit of Commodore Perry to the shores of Japan made this determination on the part of the Shogun impracticable. Bowing before the firm resolution of Perry and formidable appearance of the "black ships," the officials of the Shogun agreed to accept from Perry the letter written by President Fillmore requesting the opening of Japan to foreign intercourse and trade relations. The American commodore departed after receiving a promise that the Shogunate would respond to the American note in the following year.

Recognizing that the matter was of utmost gravity, a retainer of the Shogun, Abe Masahiro, took the unprecedented step of transmitting the President's letter to the Mikado and to the Daimyos for their consideration. Before the Shogunate could arrive at any definite decision, the impatient Commodore Perry and his squadron of seven men-of-war reappeared off Uraga in February, 1854, to demand a reply to the President's request. While the Shogunate kept stalling, the American fleet unceremoniously sailed deep into Yedo Bay. This daring movement so disconcerted the Shogunate that it was compelled to hurriedly agree to negotiations at Kanagawa.

As mentioned previously, Commodore Perry had contemplated seizing The Ryukyu Islands or the Bonin Islands on his way to Japan, but the change of presidents—from Fillmore, a Republican, to Franklin Pierce, a Democrat—completely changed the situation. Perry's earlier recommendations for aggressive actions were categorically rejected by President Pierce.

Thus, a complete reversal in the line of approach by Perry became imperative. He had now to bargain with the government in Yedo in the following vein: "Judging by the situation in East Asia, there is growing danger that Great Britain and France will encroach upon Japan. It is hardly likely that Japan, enjoying the blessings of peace for 300 years under the benign rule of the Tokugawas, is prepared to engage these powers in open hostilities. Hence, in order to remove any pretext for war, it is of great importance for Japan to make whatever concessions that are necessary as speedily as possible. This being the case, it would be prudent for Japan to conclude a treaty of friendship and commerce with the United States which harbors no territorial ambitions towards Japan. If this advice is heeded, there need be no fear of the intentions of Great Britain for she could hardly demand more than a treaty similar to that entered into with the United States."

The epoch-making negotiations between the representatives of Japan and America, commencing on March 10, 1854, were concluded on March 31, resulting in the signing of the historic Japan-United States Treaty of Friendship or the so-called Treaty of Kanagawa. This treaty, the first to swing open the secluded doors of Japan, provided for the opening of two ports, Shimoda and Hakodate, at which fuel and fresh water would be furnished to visiting mariners. It was also agreed under the "most-favored-nation" clause that any additional rights granted by Japan to another power shall also be conferred on the United States.

No sooner had the news of Perry's triumph in concluding the Treaty of Kanagawa reached Europe than England and Holland demanded the conclusion of similar treaties. These treaties were subsequently made. In due course, Admiral Poutiatine reappeared and successfully induced the Shogunate to sign a treaty with Russia, in which for the first time the principle of extraterritoriality was stipulated. The United States, as a matter of course under the most-favored-nation clause prescribed in the Treaty of Kanagawa, also received this privilege.

In accordance with the Treaty of Kanagawa, Townsend Harris arrived on board the U.S.S. Jacinto at Shimoda in September, 1856, to establish the first American Consulate General at Gyokusenji in Shimoda, aloft from which he raised the first Stars and Stripes to flutter in Japan. It was here also that the famed tale of Tojin Okichi, alleged mistress of Townsend Harris, found its origin.

In June, 1857, Harris succeeded in concluding the Treaty of Shimoda as a prelude to a treaty of commerce and trade. Then in October, Harris was received by the thirteenth Shogun, Tokugawa Iyesada, in the Yedo Castle, on which occasion Harris formally presented President Pierce's message to the Shogun.

Five days later, Harris, conferring with Lord Hotta Masamutsu, a *rochu,* eloquently explained the world situation and strongly emphasized the necessity of concluding a treaty of commerce and trade as soon as possible. "Taking advantage of the 'Arrow Incident,' both England and France are at war with China," explicated Harris. "Should the two powers prove victorious over China, they might eventually turn their attention on Japan, which would then be faced with a most dangerous situation. Therefore," he argued, "it would be to Japan's decided advantage to speedily sign a treaty with the United States and at the same time utilize America's influence to place restraints on England and France."

Accordingly, in July, 1858, the so-called Treaty of Ansei (Japan-United States Treaty of Amity and Commerce) was concluded. This treaty, opened up the four new ports of Kanagawa, Nagasaki, Niigata, and Hyogo, and retained extraterritorial rights for Americans in Japan. As there was no stipulation for customs autonomy, the treaty was unequal in character. The Treaty of Shimoda spurred the other Western powers—Holland, Russia, England and France—to demand similar treaties of commerce in rapid succession. These were subsequently inked.

Since the Treaty of Ansei was concluded by *tairo,* Ii Naosuke on behalf of the Shogunate without Imperial sanction and against the clamoring opposition, the outcry to "revere the Emperor and expel the foreigner" grew even more vociferous. Instead of placating the opposition factions, Tairo Ii adopted a policy of suppression, culminating in the so-called "mass executions of the Ansei Era." But Tairo Ii, one snowy morning in March, 1860, was himself the victim of assassination by a small band of Mito ronins at the entrance of Sakurada Gate as he was making his way to the Shogun's palace.

As was inevitable, a rising tide of anti-foreignism again began to sweep the nation, with samurai attacks on foreigners causing many casualties. In September, 1862, a group of samurais belonging to the Satsuma clan killed an Englishman and wounded two others at Namamugi on the Tokaido Highway near Kanagawa. This incident so thoroughly aroused the British that they dispatched a fleet against the Satsuma clan headquarters, bombarding and levelling a section of the city of Kagoshima. Violent anti-foreign sentiments also prompted the Choshu clan to send cannon balls hurtling against foreign vessels plying the Straits of Shimonoseki. Retaliatory bombardments upon Shimonoseki by a combined American, British, French, and Dutch squadron forced the Choshu clan into submission.

Deploring the frequency of the bloody incidents involving attacks by ronins against the foreigners, Rochu Ando Masanobu declared despairingly: "If you ronins must quench your irrepressible passions with blood, kill me or even do away with the Shogun in a rebellion, but do not precipitate a national crisis by taking the lives of foreigners!" But by this time, Great Britain, correctly concluding that the days of the Shoguns were numbered, began to visualize a united Japan under Imperial rule, backed by the leading Satsuma and Choshu clans. On the other hand, France still persisted in its support of the Yedo government. This difference in stand naturally complicated the situation, but it was already becoming increasingly evident that the once powerful Shogunate was nearing its collapse.

Revision of
Unequal Treaties

CONVINCED that it was no longer possible to effectively govern the country, the 15th Shogun, Tokugawa Yoshinobu, restored civil and military powers to the Imperial Court. In November, 1867, Emperor Meiji proclaimed the termination of the Shogunate and the restoration—after nearly 300 years—of Imperial rule.

Including the five Treaty of Ansei nations, Japan had entered into unequal treaties with sixteen nations. Since its inception, the cardinal principle of the Meiji government had been to negotiate for a revision of unequal treaties. Toward this end, succeeding Cabinets and Foreign Ministers exerted untiring efforts over an extended period.

There were two main points at issue in the unequal treaties. The first, related to extraterritoriality, was the problem of consular jurisdiction. Possessing no right to try foreign criminals in domestic courts, however serious their misdeeds, the Japanese government had to hand the criminals over to the consuls of the powers concerned for trial. The second point was the lack of customs autonomy, which prevented Japan from independently levying duties on imported goods. The actual duty was unreasonably low, being restricted to approximately 5 per cent of the value of the goods. This lack of customs autonomy naturally seriously handicapped the government's efforts to protect indigenous industries. Despite budgetary shortages, the Finance Ministry could not look to customs duties for augmenting the national income. It is no exaggeration to state, therefore, that it was the foreign powers that monopolized the profits from foreign trade.

In February, 1868, the Meiji government issued an Imperial Ordinance in which the government expressed its desire for friendly international relations but, at the same time, clearly indicated its intentions to work for the revision of the unequal treaties. In December of the same year the government, in pursuance of its avowed aims, unofficially proposed to the Ministers of Great Britain, Italy, France, America, Holland, and Germany that the treaties of 1858 should be revised in the light of the changed circumstances.

Although the government initially intended to hold the negotiations in Tokyo, it soon became apparent that there were many difficulties that had to be surmounted. It was felt that a special mission should first visit the various countries with which Japan had treaty relations, inspecting local conditions and ascertaining first-hand the views of the governments concerned. This mission, led by Iwakura Tomomi and assisted by a number of statesmen, was organized and dispatched to America and Europe in November, 1871.

Negotiations were initiated in Washington in March, 1872, but it was not until twenty-two years later in July, 1894, that the first treaty based on equality—the Anglo-Japanese Treaty of Commerce and Navigation—was signed in London. Throughout these long years, Japan's successive foreign ministers never ceased, either at international conferences or in bilateral talks, to press for equal status.

Internally, in order to strengthen Japan's position for the revision of unequal treaties, the government felt the acute need to demonstrate that Japan was a civilized and enlightened nation. The government even took such drastic action as fostering the adoption of Western manners and customs among the people. Symbolizing this new trend was the Rokumei-kan constructed in Hibiya, Tokyo, in 1883, as a social center where Japanese and foreigners gathered to enjoy evening parties and balls. This attempt to show the West that Japanese were equally civilized, became known as the Rokumei-kan era.

At the same time, genuine efforts were made to substantially improve the Japanese civil, commercial and criminal laws along Western lines. Moreover, so as to be prepared for the abolition of consular jurisdiction, the government took active steps to improve prison accommodations for foreign prisoners. With the proclamation of the Constitution in 1889 and the establishment of the Diet, Japan's rapid process of democratization went another step forward. All the while however, the nation continued to advocate treaty revisions.

Although it was the United States that first forced Japan to end her seclusion, during the four years from 1861 to 1865, she was unable to pay much heed to developments in Japan, engaged as she was in the great Civil War. Britain, which took over the predominant role in Japan, was opposed to any revision of the treaties because of her vast commercial interests and her responsibilities in India and other colonies in the Far East.

In Europe, meanwhile, Germany, Austria, and Italy, in 1882, concluded the Triple Alliance, followed in 1893 by the counterbalancing Russo-French Alliance. On the heels of this new alliance, the Russian government proclaimed throughout the realm the projected construction of the Trans-Siberian Railway, and with the aid of France, began to extend her influence in East Asia. It had long been Russia's traditional policy to acquire an ice-free port in the Southern Sea. This Russian ambition led to the Crimean War (1853–1856) and her defeat at the hands of the combined British and French forces. Despite Russia's victory over Turkey in the Russo-Turkish War (1877–1878), the determined Russian drive southward, including the control of the Balkans and advance to Constantinople, was frustrated by German machinations. No longer able to exploit her position in Turkey, Russia switched her full attention towards the Far East. Encouraged by Russia, France also joined in the scramble to expand her colonial interests in the East.

It is not surprising, therefore, that Great Britain, with vast colonial possessions in the Far East and with a preponderance of interests in China, should have viewed with deep misgivings the expansionist policies of Russia and France, particularly that of the former. Britain, suspecting that the Russian and French ministers in Tokyo were conniving with the Japanese government in a united effort to isolate Britain, felt that Japan might be tempted to participate in such a conspiracy. In view of these circumstances, Great Britain, which had hitherto opposed and consistently blocked efforts for treaty revision, staged a dramatic about-face, indicating that she was willing to moderate her policy with regard to Japan's demands. Together with this change of policy, Britain attempted to assist Japan in becoming a strong, self-supporting and independent nation.

With the removal of a major stumbling block, the Anglo-

Japanese Treaty of Commerce and Navigation was signed in London in July, 1894, significantly nine days prior to the Sino-Japanese naval engagement off Hoto. This treaty of equality between Japan and England eliminated extra-territoriality from its provisions. Although customs autonomy was not fully restored until the conclusion of the second Anglo-Japanese Treaty of Commerce and Navigation in April, 1911, it was nevertheless a promising beginning for Japan's quest for revising all existing unequal treaties. Modified treaties to restore equality between Japan on the one hand, and America, Germany, and France on the other, followed in quick succession.

Lord Kimberly, who was then British Minister of Foreign Affairs, evaluating the treaty highly, declared on the occasion that Japan's acquisition of equal status with the Western Powers was of far more significance and value than her military victory over the numerically superior Chinese army in Korea. He also voiced Britain's desire to increase friendly ties with Japan.

CHAPTER

3

The Sino-Japanese War
and the Triple
Intervention

THE SINO-JAPANESE WAR broke out in July, 1894. The interests of newly emerging Japan and those of China, the only dominant power in East Asia, had been at loggerheads over the questions of Korea, the Ryukyu Islands, and Formosa. The antagonism and confrontation between the two powers had taken on an increasingly grave overtone in Korea, regarded as a vassal by China on the one hand, and championed as an independent state by Japan on the other.

Finally in May, 1894, the Tong Hak Tong or the Society of Eastern Learning, whose avowed aim was to resist foreign influences, especially Christianity, rose up in rebellion. This incident supplied the pretext, under the terms of the Tientsin Covenant signed in April, 1885, by Japan and China, for the two powers to dispatch their troops to Korea. So strained were the relations between Japan and China that this further aggravation resulted in open hostilities between the opposing forces.

At the outset of the Sino-Japanese War, the leading powers, Great Britain, Russia, America, France, and Germany, expected China to triumph over Japan. Contrary to

25

their expectations, however, the Japanese navy defeated the Chinese fleet in the first naval engagement off the coast of Hoto. The Japanese land forces, meanwhile, scored a series of decisive victories at Songhwan and Asan, inflicting crippling blows on the enemy in subsequent battles.

As it became apparent to China that the tide of war was irreversible, the Chinese sued for peace, affixing after prolonged negotiations its signature to the Treaty of Shimonoseki in April, 1895.

The terms of the Treaty of Shimonoseki provided for the following provisions: (1) China to recognize the full and complete independence of Korea; (2) China to cede to Japan Liaotung Peninsula, Formosa, and the Pescadores; (3) China to pay an indemnity of 200,000,000 taels; (4) China to open up a specified section of the Yangtze River to Japanese commerce and the ports of Shasi, Chungking, Soochow, Hangchow to Japanese trade; (5) China to grant to Japanese subjects in China the most-favored-nation privileges.

Thus, Japan received an indemnity of 200,000,000 taels from the Sino-Japanese War and another 30,000,000 taels in compensation for the restoration of the Liaotung Peninsula to China as a result of the "Triple Intervention," or a total of 230,000,000 taels. According to German diplomatic documents published later, it was revealed that Kaiser Wilhelm II, astonished at the meager indemnity, declared that the entire amount could only be a fraction of the costs incurred by Japan in winning the war. Objectively speaking, it can be easily understood that the Japanese demands were far from being unreasonable.

The conclusion of the Treaty of Shimonoseki was greeted with extreme jubilation in Japan. Before the ink on the treaty had time to dry, a sudden turn of events in the form of the so-called "Triple Intervention" threatened to deprive Japan of the fruits of her hard won victory. A chronology of the events which ensued in the wake of the unexpected intervention proved to be one of the most agonizing chapters in Japan's diplomatic history.

Under the terms of the Treaty of Shimonoseki, China was to have ceded Liaotung Peninusla to Japan, but Russia, France, and Germany—with the Kaiser at the helm—suggested that in the interest of peace in East Asia, the Liaotung Peninsula should be restored to China. This fatal blow was delivered only six days after the signing of the Treaty of Shimonoseki and three days after the treaty was ratified by Japan.

The alarming development shocked and dismayed the nation. To cope with the serious situation, an urgent conference was convened in the presence of the Emperor in Hiroshima on April 24, 1895, a day after Japan received the three-power notification. The Premier, Count Ito Hirobumi, explained to the conference that Japan would have to adopt one of three alternatives. The three courses open to Japan were: (1) reject the three power "advice" even at the risk of inviting their enmity; (2) refer the issue to an international conference; or (3) accept the "advice" and restore the territory in question to China.

In the course of the heated deliberations, the conference decided tentatively in favor of submitting the whole question to an international conference. However, before reaching a final decision, Premier Ito, accompanied by Finance Minister Matsukata and Home Minister Nomura, hurried to Maiko to solicit the views of Foreign Minister Count Mutsu who was then recuperating from an illness.

The tentative decision of the Hiroshima Conference met with Count Mutsu's vigorous opposition. With unusual persuasion, he argued that the convening of such a conference would not only require a great deal of time but would also aggravate unnecessarily the already complex

international situation. Moreover, he felt that such a conference might engender a whole series of questions in connection with the treaty and might even cause the entire
structure of the treaty itself to collapse once the great powers
engaged in bickerings over their own national interests.

In the face of such persuasive arguments, the Premier
could not help but accept the views of Count Mutsu, and
adopted a modified policy of "conceding to the three powers,
but remaining firm with China."

In other words, Japan decided to negotiate with flex-
ibility, prepared to listen to the views of the three powers,
but insofar as China was concerned, to pursue a policy of
no concession. At the same time, Japan set her mind on
feeling out the attitudes of the other powers, in the pursuance of which the government instructed Kato, the Japanese
Minister in London, to ascertain how far Great Britain was
prepared to go to help Japan in meeting the critical situation.

Following a cabinet meeting, the British Minister for
Foreign Affairs, Lord Kimberley, outlined his government's
stand as follows: "Great Britain has no objection to the
Japanese possession of Formosa, but feels that the act of
interceding in behalf of Japan would also be regarded as
intervention. Furthermore, Britain entertains some doubts
as to whether it would be prudent in the interests of Japan's
future for her to acquire a toe hold on the mainland. Not
only would Japan have to increase her military expenditures
to maintain such a possession, but she might also incur the
potential danger of China and Russia embarking upon a
war of revenge. In these circumstances, it might be more
judicious for Japan to adopt a conciliatory attitude."

Through its Minister in Washington, Kurino, the Japanese government also received a negative reply not unlike
that of Great Britain. Japan was informed that the United

States had no clash of interests with Russia. With only Italy expressing a desire to support Japan, all hopes of relying on the support of other powers were completely dashed.

Elated over Japan's failure to win effective support in countering the Triple Intervention, China proposed the postponement of the exchange of ratifications. In its attitude towards China, however, Japan continued to adhere to the position of upholding the provisions of the Treaty of Shimonoseki.

Subsequently released German diplomatic documents clearly bear out the fact that the partition of China was being contemplated, and France had designs over Formosa. In the view of these circumstances, it was wise for Japan to have rejected the idea of an international conference to discuss the Triple Intervention.

In retrospect, Japan in renouncing her claims to the Liaotung Peninsula, should have placed China under treaty obligation not to lease the said territory to a third power. The failure to do this must be regarded as a Japanese diplomatic blunder. Be that as it may, Japan had amply demonstrated her prowess in arms by decisively winning the Sino-Japanese War, thus establishing herself internationally as a great East Asiatic power.

As explained earlier, Russia's advance in the East caused Great Britain to draw closer to Japan. It was to maintain the balance of power in East Asia and to protect her vital interests that Britain endeavored to make the best use of victorious Japan, though she was as yet unprepared to consider the conclusion of an alliance with Japan. More important to her was the alliance with China to check the Russian eastward thrust. Any thoughts she might have entertained at the time for an alliance with Japan were only as a supplement to the Anglo-Chinese alliance.

In short, Britain, recognizing that her interests were

similar to those of China, overestimated the strength of the Far Eastern colossus. This British attitude persisted until the early stages of the Sino-Japanese War. Although not an exception in anticipating the defeat of Japan in the Sino-Japanese War, Britain believed that her paramount interest lay not in the question of whether China or Japan would emerge triumphant from the war but, rather, the need to resist Russia's attempts to take advantage of the conflict to expand Russian influence in Asia.

Britain, therefore, on a number of occasions suggested to both Japan and China that she was ready to act as an arbitrator to bring the hostilities to an end, hoping thereby to protect her commercial interests in China. But Japan's successive victories opened the eyes of the British to the fact that it was in their interest to seek future alliance not with China, but with Japan, for the maintenance of stability in Asia, and the Far East in particular.

Choice Between
Great Britain
and Russia

OR NEARLY ten years prior to the outbreak of the
Russo-Japanese War, the foreign policy of Japan had
two principal targets. The bitter lesson of the "Triple
Intervention" had convinced Japan that any victory in the
battlefield would have to be secured by a corresponding
triumph in the field of diplomacy. Japan was finding herself
increasingly in a position where she could not allow Russian
penetration of Manchuria and Korea to go unchallenged,
not only on grounds of national security, but politically and
economically. She would either have to choose between
reaching an understanding with Russia, on the basis of
which the stability of Asia would be safeguarded, or join
with Great Britain in a common cause to halt the Russian
juggernaut. Immediately after the Triple Intervention, the
Japanese government came face to face with the painful
decision of either reaching some detente with Russia or ally-
ing itself with Great Britain.

Among the Russophiles in Japan were Marquis Ito and
Marquis Yamagata, backed by the powerful group of
genro, who formed the main current of the Japanese
government at the time. This powerful group was opposed

31

by a minority faction—centering around Takaaki Kato, then Japanese Minister to London and later Foreign Minister—which energetically advocated an Anglo-Japanese alliance. Kato was strongly encouraged by Joseph Chamberlain, Secretary of State for the Colonies in the Salisbury Cabinet, with whom he was in frequent contact, that Japan should act courageously against Russian ambitions. Convinced of the soundness of this argument, Kato repeatedly urged the Japanese government to adopt a firm policy against Russia.

The main current group, with Marquis Ito as the moving spirit, however, wished to reach some understanding with Russia, believing that the British position in the world was gradually waning. They emphasized the growing unwillingness of Great Britain to adopt a firm policy, similar to the one she had adopted in 1861 when she dispatched two warships to Tsushima to force the Russian fleet to evacuate its occupation of the island. Furthermore, Britain was internationally in a position of isolation.

In order to attain this understanding, Marquis Ito proposed his famous "exchange policy," an issue on which both parties engaged in prolonged but fruitless negotiations. The policy involved Russian recognition of Japan's sphere of influence in Korea in exchange for Japanese recognition of Russia's sphere of influence in Manchuria. While Russia welcomed Japan's proposal to renounce her interests in China, it could not recognize Japan's position of predominance in Korea, militarily and politically. Hence, the exchange plan fell through.

At the beginning, Russia's ambitious Far Eastern policy was one of vagueness. But followng her success in compelling Japan to renounce her claim to the Liaotung Peninsula, Russian policy underwent a complete reversal, becoming not only positive but aggressive. In September, 1896, Russia and China concluded the Li-Lobanoff Secret Alliance, directed against Japan, under which the former acquired the right to construct a railroad across northern Manchuria to Vladivostok. The Russian tentacles quickly extended beyond Manchuria into Korea, and in the following year Russia exacted mining and lumbering rights in the strategic peninsula. The Russians then pressured Korea to employ Russian military and financial advisers, and attempted to acquire Masampo at the southern-extremity of Korea.

Finally, she extended her ambitions into the Liaotung Peninsula, from which Japan had earlier been ousted as a result of the Triple Intervention, her fleet occupying Port Arthur and Talien in December, 1897. In March, 1898, the Russians went even further, forcing China to sign the treaty leasing Kwantung Province. This Russian aggrandizement was naturally supported by her French allies, and Germany had already secured Kiaochow. France soon followed suit by leasing Kwangchow Bay, and Britain obtained the lease of Weihaiwei and Kowloon. The inevitable partitioning of China by the great powers had started.

In spite of these tense developments, Japan continued perseveringly to negotiate with Russia on the principle of the "exchange policy." In 1900, however, taking advantage of the Boxer Uprising in China, Russian troops occupied the whole of Manchuria. Large numbers of Russian soldiers also began infiltrating into north China in an attempt to intimidate Japan. Realizing the futility of reaching a compromise with Russia, opinion in Japan slowly turned in favor of the Anglo-Japanese alliance.

Britain, on the other hand, was grappling with the international situation which made her traditional foreign policy of "glorious isolation" no longer tenable. Her "isolation" was being seriously challenged in all parts of the world. Britain's predominant position in China was being menaced by Russia's southward advance. Unless China's independence and sovereignty were guaranteed, Britain feared that she would lose not only her markets in China, but also find it extremely difficult to maintain her footholds in Hong Kong, Malaya and Burma. A Russian attack against India would also become possible.

Having written off her former policy of isolation as a failure, Britain began to actively seek alliances with other powers. As a first step, Britain unsuccessfully tried to reach some rapprochement with Russia over China and the Near and Middle East regions. Her attempt to sound out Germany on an alliance also met with a similar rebuff. Japan, the only other great power in the Far East, naturally became the next target of Britain's approaches for an alliance.

The First Anglo-
Japanese Treaty
of Alliance

THE LONG-AWAITED First Anglo-Japanese Alliance was concluded in January, 1902. The epochal document consisted only of a preamble and six articles. In the preamble the two contracting powers, Japan and Great Britain, affirmed their determination to uphold the "independence and territorial integrity of the Empire of China and the Empire of Korea," and to secure "equal opportunities in those countries for the commerce and industry of all nations."

In the text of the alliance, the two powers defined their respective interests, those of Great Britain, relating principally to China, while those of Japan relating to China specifically stating in a peculiar degree, politically as well as commercially and industrially," and to Korea recognizing the right of taking "such measures as may be indispensable in order to safeguard those interests if threatened by the aggressive action of any other powers."

In case either Great Britain or Japan, in defense of their respective interests, should become involved in war with another power, the other "will maintain a strict neutrality, and use its efforts to prevent other powers from joining in hostilities against its ally," but, should any other power or powers enter the war, the other "will come to its assistance, will conduct war in common." In other words, in case Japan should become involved in war with Russia, and France, Russia's ally, should join in hostilities against Japan, Great Britain would conduct war in common. Moreover, they agreed to communicate with each other fully and frankly whenever their interests were considered to be in jeopardy. The alliance was to remain in force for five years.

The Anglo-Japanese Alliance raised Japan to the status of a great power and was effective as a lever in applying pressure against Russia. Taking advantage of its importance, Japan attempted to carry through her fundamental "exchange policy" principle. In essence, as far as Japan was concerned, the Anglo-Japanese Alliance was not necessarily a treaty of alliance for the purpose of waging hostilities against Russia, but a treaty providing a strong backing in future diplomatic negotiations.

Needless to say, Russia was profoundly displeased and disconcerted by the Anglo-Japanese Treaty of Alliance. Consequently, Russia, together with France, issued a joint declaration on March 16, 1902, in a bold demonstration against the treaty. Meanwhile, the Anglo-Japanese Alliance had a salutary effect. On April 8, 1902, two months after the Alliance was concluded, the Russo-Chinese Convention regarding Manchuria was signed, providing among other things for the gradual withdrawal of Russian forces from Manchuria.

The Russo-
Japanese War

IN CONFORMITY with the Russo-Chinese Convention regarding Manchuria of April 8, 1902, Russia faithfully completed the first stage of the evacuation in May, 1902. However, as the agreed date for the second stage of the evacuation drew near, far from showing any disposition to fulfill the terms of the Convention, Russia not only sent troops into south Manchuria, an area she had never before occupied, but also presented seven demands to the Chinese government that would place Manchuria under the protection of the Russian government. Furthermore, ignoring the vigorous protests lodged by Japan, Great Britain and the United States, Russia continued her penetration, occupying the entire area around the mouth of the Yalu River.

Negotiations between Japan and Russia began at St. Petersburg between Kurino, the Japanese Minister, and Lamsdorff, the Russian Minister for Foreign Affairs. In persuance of the principle of the "exchange policy," Japan adopted a conciliatory and frank spirit in her consultations with the Russian government with a view to dissolving the differences that were causing concern to the two governments. In contrast to Japan's attitude, Russia not only did not show any sincerity in making concessions over the Korean problem, but even refused to negotiate on the question of Manchuria. Although Japan exerted every effort to settle the issues peacefully through diplomatic means, the Russian government on one pretext or another failed to reply to Japan's repeated inquiries.

During this period, she continued her diversionary tactics, suddenly evacuating her forces from Manchuria, and just as suddenly dispatching reinforcements into the area. Throughout the frustrating negotiations between Japan and Russia, the British government was kept fully informed by Japan.

Great Britain, while fully supporting the position of the Japanese government, had no intention of encouraging Japan either to enter into hostilities with Russia, or to recommend that Japan compromise with Russia. Britain's main preoccupation was to abide faithfully by the provisions of the alliance and to extend to Japan the maximum assistance possible consistent with her obligations. It was under such circumstances that Japan formally declared war against Russia on February 10, 1904.

When Japan made her momentous decision to enter into a state of war with Russia, she did so without any expectation of military assistance from Great Britain. On the other hand, she did request economic and financial assistance which her European ally willingly provided. The United States government, too, extended economic assistance to Japan. These foreign loans, mostly from Britain and America, constituted a very important part of the Japanese government's resources in defraying the cost of war.

Needless to say, the war with Russia was an event of the first magnitude for Japan, a veritable life and death struggle for the small island nation pitted against a colossus. Following a series of sensational but costly victories, Japan's land

and sea forces emerged triumphant from the crucial conflict. Despite the military successes, Japan responded favorably to the initiative taken by President Theodore Roosevelt of the United States to act as a peace-maker. Having received Russian willingness to conclude a treaty of peace with Japan, President Roosevelt was able to bring the two warring nations around the conference table in Portsmouth in August, 1905.

Prior to this conference, Japan had dispatched Baron Kaneko Kentaro, a classmate of President Roosevelt at Yale University, to the United States to discuss details of the peace negotiations with the United States government. Consequently, the framework of the Portsmouth Treaty had already been drawn up when the two plenipotentiaries, Komura and Witte, began preliminary talks. The Portsmouth Treaty was subsequently signed on September 5, 1905, recognizing Japan's paramount political, military and economic interests in Korea as well as her right of guidance, protection and control in case she deemed it necessary. Japan also inherited the Russian leases of the Leased Territory of Kwantung, wherein both Port Arthur and Talien are situated, and the railways south of Changchun, a point dividing north and south Manchuria, with all rights and privileges pertaining thereto—providing China's acquiescence was first obtained.

Although a demand for payment of an indemnity was rejected by Russia, Japan acquired the southern half of Sakhalin, south of latitude 50°N, and the payment of ¥80,000,000 for having taken care of a tremendous number of Russian prisoners of war.

The Russo-Japanese War established Japan's undisputed position among the foremost powers in the world, greatly heightening her national glory. As a result of her unbroken record of military triumphs and the Portsmouth Treaty,

Japan succeeded in expelling Russian influence from Korea and from the south of Manchuria. Shortly thereafter, Japan concluded the Treaty of Peking with China in December, 1905, which granted Japan her first firm foothold on the Asiatic continent through the Chinese transfer of both the Russian leases of the Leased Territory of Kwantung and the South Manchurian Railway. Japan was also able to look forward to trade expansion in north China.

By demonstrating her national strength, Japan ushered in a new age of equal relations with the Western powers in China. In the meantime, Japan had been negotiating with Great Britain for the renewal of the Anglo-Japanese Alliance which was to expire in 1907. Thus, the Second Anglo-Japanese Alliance was finalized just prior to the consummation of the Russo-Japanese peace negotiations. In addition, the Franco-Japanese Agreement, the Russo-Japanese Agreement (both in 1907) and the Root-Takahira Agreement (1908) were concluded, by which Japan firmly established her position of security.

Attitude of
the United States

THE UNITED STATES attitude toward Japan was unquestionably sympathetic until the latter—to the amazement of the world—emerged victorious from the Russo-Japanese War. Throughout the critical period of the hostilities, President Roosevelt displayed a feeling of amity toward Japan, even going so far as to offer his good offices to mediate in the peace parley between Japan and Russia. But with Japan's growing national strength following the war, this benign attitude gradually changed to one of fear and anxiety.

The United States had earlier annexed Hawaii in 1897, and emerged from the Spanish-American War in possession of the Philippine Islands in 1898. With these territorial acquisitions, America lost no time in embarking on a definitive and positive policy in the Far East. In September, 1899, John Hay, the U.S. Secretary of State, proclaimed an epochal doctrine on China, affirming the principles of the open door and equal trading opportunities. By formally informing Japan of this declaration of policy in December, the United States made known its intention to exercise a dominating role as a Far Eastern power.

In the years that followed the Russo-Japanese War, Japanese immigration to the United States increased rapidly. By 1907, the number of immigrants had exceeded 30,000. To stem the rising tide of Japanese immigration, Japan and America entered into a so-called "gentlemen's agreement" in December, 1907, under which the Japanese government agreed to cooperate with the United States government in jointly controlling immigration and voluntarily prohibiting the further immigration of Japanese laborers into the United States.

In spite of this measure, discrimination against the Japanese in California continued unabated. It was under such circumstances that the United States dispatched its Pacific fleet to East Asian waters, ostensibly to visit the Philippine Islands. However, the warships always made it a practice to call at Japan's ports at the "invitation" of the Japanese government. The real purpose of these frequent calls was undoubtedly to demonstrate American naval presence in the Pacific.

An inspiring idea in connection with railway interests in Manchuria, which took shape in the mind of an ambitious individual, and which was far removed from U.S. government involvement, sparked off a series of consequential events. This was the enterprising plan of the American railway tycoon, Edward H. Harriman, father of Averell Harriman, current Undersecretary of State for Political Affairs, to purchase railway rights in Manchuria. Mr. Harriman had a long cherished and abiding interest in the Far East. The South Manchuria Railway was the first target upon which he fixed his covetous eyes. He envisaged a round-the-world transportation system, based on the acquisition of the right to manage the said railway, the purchase of the Chinese Eastern Railway, and the procurement of the right of passage over the West Siberian Railway which would reach the Baltic Sea, then extend further westwards across the Atlantic Ocean to link up with the American transcontinental railway over which he had controlling interests.

With this grandiose scheme in mind, Harriman came to Japan in August, 1905, and in his interviews with Premier Count Katsura and the *genro,* laid out his plan for a joint Japanese American control of the South Manchuria Railway. Completely swept off their feet by this fabulous proposal, both Premier Katsura and Finance Minister Inouye expressed their readiness to share in this joint venture, hoping thereby to kill two birds with one stone. By selling Japanese interests in the railway, it would be possible, on one hand, to rescue Japan from her war-caused financial plight and, on the other, an American-controlled railway in Manchuria would provide a buffer zone against Russia, forestalling any attempt by Russia to embark upon a war of revenge. Accordingly, the Katsura-Harriman provisional memorandum was signed in October, 1905. Highly elated over the successful outcome of the first stage of his plan to establish a global transportation system, Harriman exultantly left Japan for America, little suspecting that all his dreams were soon to be dashed.

Foreign Minister Komura, who was to deliver this coup de grace, was at the time on the high seas en route home from the Portsmouth Peace Conference. When acquainted with the details of the Harriman proposal on board the vessel, Komura could hardly control his profound anger. Komura not only objected to the plan of joint management, but charged the government with gross indiscretion for having attempted to relinquish the only tangible asset gained by Japan from the Russo-Japanese War. Firmly convinced that he was acting in the national interest, Komura, on arriving home, tried to persuade the Premier, the Cabinet members, and the *genro,* to nullify the provisional agreement. Baron Komura's forceful contentions finally swayed Prince Katsura and his Cabinet to decide in favor of renouncing the Katsura-Harriman provisional memorandum, thereby retaining Japan's acquired rights in Manchuria. Harriman, who had already returned to San Francisco, was notified accordingly and persuaded to accept the change in Japan's decision.

Despite Japan's unilateral decision to renounce the Katsura-Harriman provisional memorandum, America could not and did not forget the fact that the Japanese government had at one time expressed its willingness to allow Japanese and American capitalists to share in the joint management of undertakings in Manchuria. It is important to bear this fact in mind for a better understanding of American policy toward Manchuria in later years.

American policy in Manchuria took another significant turn in November, 1909, when Philander Knox, Secretary of State in the Taft Administration, offered a proposal to Great Britain, France, Germany, Russia and Japan, known ever since as the "Knox Neutralization Plan for Manchurian Railways." Japan, whose sphere of influence was then confined to south Manchuria, and Russia, whose sphere of influence lay in north Manchuria, decided, after mutual consultation, to refuse the American proposal separately. In accordance with their understanding, Japan delivered her objections to the United States government.

About two years prior to the American move, the First Russo-Japanese agreement—The Motono-Iswalsky Agreement—containing secret clauses, had already been signed between Japan and Russia in 1907, in which both nations professed common purposes to protect their interests.

As a consequence of the Russo-Japanese War, Japan gained a strong foothold in the Far East and elevated her status to that of one of the great powers of the East. The direction of American Far Eastern policy, however, inevitably led to a collision of interests between Japan and the United States. On the other hand, China, with a view to lessening the influence of both Japan and Russia, tried to induce America to intervene in the problems of Manchuria, and, in furtherance of its designs, encouraged the introduction into Manchuria of foreign capital from the Western powers.

As has been previously stated, Japan's foreign policy, with the Anglo-Japanese Alliance as its cornerstone, was based on respect for Chinese independence and territorial integrity as well as the principles of the open door and equal opportunity. Since John Hay had enunciated a similar doctrine with regard to China, Japan indirectly recognized the United States as a friendly nation. The Russo-Japanese War was itself the natural outcome of Japan's efforts to defend her purposes and principles. However, the Knox Neutralization Plan for Manchurian Railways impelled both Japan and Russia to align themselves against America, motivated as they were by a common desire to safeguard their special interests in Korea, Manchuria, and Inner Mongolia.

Nevertheless, the dominating view of Foreign Minister Komura and other leaders of the Japanese government was in favor of maintaining friendly relations with the leading naval powers, such as Great Britain and America, as Japan's fundamental principle of foreign policy. The Russo-Japanese cooperation, on the other hand, was regarded as only a temporary expedient to defend Japan's vital interests in Korea, Manchuria, and Inner Mongolia. The conclusion of the Root-Takahira Agreement in November, 1908, the aim of which was to insure the peace of the Pacific, is convincing proof of this fact. But Japanese-American relations, aggravated by the problem of Japanese immigration, slowly but surely began to take an unfortunate turn for the worse.

Russo-Japanese
Agreements

WHILE THE details surrounding the Anglo-Japanese Alliance are generally well known, even the Japanese public knows very little about the agreements between Japan and Russia.

The end of the Russo-Japanese War afforded both Japan and Russia with circumstances that favored cooperation between the two antagonists. Horrified by the dangerous risks that were inherent in a major war, the Japanese leaders hoped, above all, to be able to circumvent any war of vengeance by Russia.

Peace was indispensable for Japan as she strained every effort to recover from the grievous wounds inflicted by the war. In addition, in order to carry out her plans in China —the real object of Japan's policy—it was keenly realized that Russian cooperation was a prerequisite. The foundation of the policy was based on the Portsmouth Treaty.

Under these circumstances, *Genro* Yamagata and Ito saw eye to eye on the necessity of cooperating with Russia. On the other hand, in Russia, as a result of the disastrous defeat she suffered in the war against Japan, the faction favoring compromises toward Japan assumed greater influence. The appointment of Iswalsky as Minister for Foreign Affairs reflected this change of attitude.

Not unlike her adversary, Russia was also exhausted militarily and financially as a consequence of the war. Beset with internal problems, Russia no longer possessed the power to cope singly with the augmented Anglo-Japanese Alliance in the Far East. Accordingly, in order to continue carrying on her Far Eastern policy, the existence of a powerful ally became an essential precondition. Russia naturally moved in the direction of closer relations with France, her ally, but the latter had already arrived at an understanding with Great Britain—Russia's traditional enemy—in 1904, and no longer wished to expend her energy in behalf of Russia's Far Eastern policy under the Franco-Russian Alliance of 1893. Meanwhile, Germany had built up a preponderant position in Europe and the Middle East, becoming a source of grave concern to powers whose interests were directly affected. Russian attempts to woo Germany met with no success.

Having failed in her endeavors to counteract the Anglo-Japanese Alliance, Russia finally embarked on a policy of compromising with Great Britain. It was natural, however, for the Anglo-Russian Agreement to have an anti-German tinge. At the same time, Russia felt the need to obtain Japan's assurance before undertaking a bold policy in the Balkans and the Middle East. Russia's rapprochement toward Japan was welcomed by France from the standpoint of the Franco-Russian Alliance and the Anglo-French Entente Cordiale. In addition, France took the initiative to sign the Franco-Japanese Agreement in June, 1907, regulating the spheres of influence in Japan and in East Asia.

It had been mutually agreed at the time of the conclusion of the peace treaty at Portsmouth that the details would be ironed out later. With this aim in view, the two powers initiated talks in December, 1905, which lasted until December of the following year, but no progress was attained during the prolonged negotiations, much to Japan's great annoyance. The favorable turn in the diplomatic talks on an Anglo-Russian Agreement, in the meantime, spurred the progress of the Russo-Japanese talks in which Great Britain and France played a mediatory role.

One of the greatest factors to influence Russia to adopt a more conciliatory attitude and come to an understanding with Japan on the details of the Portsmouth Treaty, was the conclusion of the Franco-Japanese Agreement. Thus, in July, 1907, the two countries finally inked the documents of the first Russo-Japanese Agreement—the Motono-Iswalsky Agreement.

In the preamble of this agreement, Japan and Russia, "desiring to consolidate the relations of peace and good neighborhood which have happily been re-established between Japan and Russia, and wishing to remove for the future every cause of misunderstanding in the relations of the two Empires," agreed, in the text, "to sustain and defend the maintenance of the status quo in the Far East."

Further, in the secret convention, both parties agreed on the line of demarcation in Manchuria by which they were to sustain their mutual interests in each sphere of influence, and they mutually acknowledged Japan's free action in Korea and Russia's special interests in Outer Mongolia.

After the consummation of this agreement, the United States proposed the Neutralization Plan for Manchurian Railways and this, as previously stated, met with Japan's refusal. America's proposal concerning the Manchurian railway enterprise induced Japan and Russia to draw closer to each other over the issue of Manchuria. After repeated negotiations, the second Motono-Iswalsky Agreement was signed in July, 1910.

Under the preamble of this agreement, it ascertained that the signatory governments were sincerely attached to the principle established by the Agreement of 1907, with its effect enlarged and strengthened. Further, Japan and Russia, in the secret convention, recognized the right of taking such measures as may be indispensable in order to safeguard their special interests in their respective spheres of influence in divided Manchuria, and agreed to negotiate with one another as to the measures to be taken in order to give mutual assistance whenever their special interests were threatened by the aggressive actions of any other powers.

Feeling that conditions were opportune, Iswalsky, the Russian Minister for Foreign Affairs, lost no time in making overtures to Japan for the partition of China. Russian plans not only called for the division of China into two spheres of influence, but also for the ultimate possession of the carved territories by Japan and Russia. Japan's reaction to the Russian proposition for the partition of China was one of vigorous opposition, the reasons being that Japan agreed to respect the territorial integrity and the principle of the open door in China as set out in the Anglo-Japanese Alliance, and Japan acknowledged John Hay's declaration of 1899, proclaiming equal opportunity and the open door in China which was upheld in the Root-Takahira Agreement of 1908.

Despite these conflicting views, the third Russo-Japanese Agreement was concluded in July, 1912. This accord was stimulated by the Chinese Currency Reform Loan Agreement spearheaded by the United States and three other powers—Great Britain, France and Germany. It will be recalled that the consummation of the second Russo-Japanese Agreement was accelerated by America's Neutralization Plan for Manchurian Railways. At the time of the conclusion of the Four Power Loan Agreement, Japan reserved for herself special rights in the region of Southern Manchuria and contiguous Inner Mongolia, while Russia did the same with respect to the regions of northern Manchuria, Mongolia and Turkistan.

Through the instrument of the third Russo-Japanese Agreement, the two powers pledged to respect the regions of special interests of both nations, confirming the division of Inner Mongolia into East and West in which they would maintain separate spheres of influence, just as they did in Manchuria in 1907. The fourth Russo-Japanese Agreement was concluded in July, 1916. Unlike the earlier Russo-Japanese agreements, whether secret or open, which confined themselves to the regions of Manchuria and Mongolia, the fourth accord not only extended their spheres of influence to the whole of China, but also contained a secret provision stipulating that the two powers would wage war in common against any other power trespassing on their vital interests. The fourth agreement was, for all intents and purposes, a defensive and offensive alliance.

Thus, Japan and Russia had concluded four agreements, the last being the defensive and offensive treaty. The circumstances and the precise provisions of these treaties were not universally known until the Russian revolutionary government, in 1917, disclosed the hitherto unrevealed contents of these agreements.

CHAPTER 9

Second Anglo-Japanese Alliance

J APAN and Great Britain, mutually desirous that the First Anglo-Japanese Alliance should be extended to strengthen the existing close understanding between the two nations, concluded the Second Anglo-Japanese Alliance in August, 1905, just before the Portsmouth Treaty went into effect. The new agreement was defensive as well as offensive and broadened the application of the treaty to as far as India.

Significant was the abandonment of the neutrality clause which animated the first alliance, and its replacement by the principle of a defensive and offensive alliance, in which the contracting parties agreed that, in case Russia attacked India, Japan would come to the assistance of its ally and conduct the war in common. Similarly, in case Russia invaded Manchuria, Great Britain would rush to the assistance of its ally without delay to jointly prosecute the war.

Whereas China and Korea were regarded in the same light in the first alliance, Great Britain now specifically recognized that "Japan, possessing paramount interests in Korea, had the right to take such measures as were necessary to protect her own interests, provided that such measures

53

did not conflict with the principle of equal opportunity for the commerce and industry of all nations." It is noteworthy that the new accord clearly recognized Japan's position in Korea, acknowledging that Korea had been the bone of contention between Japan and Russia which precipitated the two countries into war. If both nations had arrived at an understanding on the "exchange of Manchuria and Korea formula," hostilities could have been averted. One of the chief objectives of this new pact was to remove this dangerous seed of armed conflict.

While the foremost aim of the First Anglo-Japanese Alliance was to forestall Japan from surrendering and to enable her to effectively resist the attacks which Russia might make singly or in concert with her allies, the Second Alliance had the objective of diverting Russia's attention away from India and East Asia toward Europe and fostering cooperation with the allied powers.

Agreement on this Second Anglo-Japanese Alliance was actually reached in the midst of the Portsmouth Peace Conference, but, anxious to avoid any act that might incite Russia into rupturing the negotiations, the announcement of the treaty was postponed until after Japan and Russia had ended their talks.

However, in order to dispel the reported misunderstanding among some German officials and individuals that the second treaty of alliance contained provisions detrimental to Germany's vested rights, Japan unofficially communicated the full text of the alliance to Chancellor Marquis von Bulow, who, on reading the text, replied that there was nothing objectionable in the treaty.

At the same time, the Japanese government also unofficially informed the French government of the nature of the treaty. In view of her position as an ally of Russia, France not only expressed gratification for the goodwill shown by Japan, but also appreciated the fact that the pact was not publicly disclosed while the peace negotiations with Russia were proceeding.

Annexation of
Korea by Japan

THE inherent weakness and corruptness of Korea, through its history from ancient times, had long been a source of deep anxiety and concern which directly jeopardized Japan's national security. It will be recalled that it was the Korean instability that led to the Sino-Japanese War, and Russia's aggressive action towards Korea that ignited the flames of war between Japan and Russia.

As soon as Japan declared war against Russia, she initiated negotiations in Seoul with the Korean government on an agreement which was concluded on February, 1904, the aim of which was to assure Japan's special position in Korea. Under this Japanese-Korean Protocol, Japan was empowered to take such necessary measures, militarily and administratively, as circumstances required, in case the welfare of the Imperial House or the territorial integrity of Korea was threatened by the aggressive action of a third power or by internal disturbances.

The next step in the growing Korean-Japanese rapprochement was taken in July, 1904, resulting in the conclusion of another agreement the following month. By October the Korean government had agreed to engage a Japanese subject

57

as "financial adviser to the Korean government." Thus, Korea—step by step—came under Japanese control, diplomatically as well as financially.

As previously stated, Japan's special predominant position in Korea was first recognized by the Second Anglo-Japanese Alliance, then by the Portsmouth Treaty, the Franco-Japanese Agreement, and finally by the Katsura-Roosevelt Understanding of August, 1905,

Subsequently, the Second Japanese-Korean Protocol was successfully concluded and signed on November 17, 1905. The new Protocol established Japan's virtual protectorate over Korea, granting Japan the control and direction of Korea's foreign relations and providing for the appointment of a Japanese Resident-General in Korea, primarily for the purpose of taking charge of and directing matters relating to diplomatic affairs. In launching this momentous policy, the Japanese government issued a statement to the powers concerned. Great Britain, the United States, China, France, Germany and Italy acquiesced, realizing the practical necessity and wisdom of Japan's procedure.

In June, 1907, the Japanese government obtained Korea's assent to the Third Japanese-Korean Agreement, placing the administration of all important state affairs, official appointments and dismissals, and the enactment of all laws and ordinances in the hands of the Japanese Resident-General. Japan thus firmly placed herself in control of the internal administration of the peninsular state.

While she strove to gain this position of pre-eminence in Korea, Japan had also succesfully worked out the details of the First Russo-Japanese Agreement which only awaited the signatures of the contracting powers before it would become effective.

Later, in July, 1909, the Ministers of the Katsura Cabinet in an important meeting, decided that Japan should annex

Korea at an appropriate time. In line with this decision, the Treaty of Annexation was concluded and signed in August, 1910, without any objection by any of the interested powers.

Third Anglo-
Japanese Alliance

FOLLOWING Japan's victory in the Russo-Japanese War, a cooling of relations between Japan and Great Britain set in as the former gradually extended her influence, both politically and commercially, into areas in the Far East hitherto regarded by Great Britain as her sphere of influence. Although their relations were still governed by the Second Anglo-Japanese Alliance, the alliance itself no longer found much public favor in Britain. Ties with the United States also took a turn for the worse on account of the Japanese immigration problem and the question of Manchuria.

While British public opinion evinced little enthusiasm for renewing the alliance, official circles led by sir Edward Grey, Minister of Foreign Affairs, continued to attach great importance to the alliance. Britain, at the time, was confronted with many serious issues, not the least of which was the growth of Germany which began to challenge British supremacy in various parts of the world.

Britain had to counter not only Germany's rising naval power, but also had to tackle the issue of Morocco, the Baghdad Railway controversy, and the problems arising out of German colonies in Africa and the South Seas. In such circumstances, many people in Britain urged the prolongation of the alliance as a means of bolstering the British position vis-a-vis Germany.

Japan, for her part, felt that the alliance, contributing to the maintenance of peace in the Far East, was not only indispensable but also beneficial for the promotion of economic expansion. Thus, four years before the expiration of the Second Anglo-Japanese Alliance, the Third Anglo-Japanese Alliance was signed on July 13, 1911.

During the negotiations for the renewal of the treaty, the British Foreign Minister, Sir Edward Grey, made it clear that the Anglo-Japanese Treaty, aimed originally at countering Russia, should in no way arouse any misunderstanding on the part of the United States. Negotiations for a general arbitration treaty were then in progress between Britain and the United States.

Consequently, the 1911 Treaty contained a very important addition that "should either of the High Contracting Parties conclude a treaty of general arbitration with a third power, it is agreed that nothing in this agreement shall impose on such contracting party an obligation to go to war with the power with whom such an arbitration treaty is in force."

Not only did the revised part place the United States outside its purview, but it eliminated the articles relating to the British recognition of Japan's special interests in Korea and Great Britain's special concern over the security of the frontiers of India.

In the light of these circumstances, it is natural to assume that Japan's foreign policy towards the United States was based more on the Russo-Japanese Agreement than on the Anglo-Japanese Alliance. That was the general situation on the eve of the outbreak of the First World War in 1914.

First World War

SHORTLY after the outbreak of World War I, in July, 1914, the British Admiralty formally requested the Japanese government to dispatch its fleet "to hunt down and, if possible, destroy the armed German merchant cruisers which were in the Far East attacking British commerce." Seizing this opportunity to participate in the war, Japan contemplated driving out Germany from Tsingtao and, at the same time, taking over its interests.

However, the British Ministry of Foreign Affairs not only did not welcome Japan's participation in the war, but even voiced its opposition to any hasty involvement. While it did not raise any objection to Japan's occupation of Tsingtao, it could not countenance any move prejudicial to China's sovereignty and independence. Moreover, she strongly opposed the creation of chaotic conditions in the Far East.

In the light of her immense interests in China, particularly in central and south China, Britain indicated her desire that Japan withhold participation in the conflict at least for the time being. Thus, whereas the British Admiralty urged Japan's immediate and active participation, the

Foreign Office in London urged a waiting policy. But as the war dragged on, the British government proposed that Japan enter the world struggle but confine itself to limited military actions, restricting its activities to German leased territories in the Far East and the Pacific Ocean.

Notwithstanding the Japanese government's rejection of this proposal, Britain unilaterally issued a statement to this effect. Japan protested, but nothing conclusive resulted from these exchanges. Thereupon, she sent an ultimatum to Germany, but receiving no reply within the time limit, Japan formally declared war against Germany on August 23, 1914, the date of expiration of the ultimatum. Japan's primary task was to capture the German naval base at Tsingtao, and Kiachow was subsequently occupied in November.

Meanwhile, the Japanese fleet captured the South Sea Islands where the Germans had established a naval base, hunted out the German warships in the Far East, and convoyed the troopships from British territories to the battle-fields of Europe. The Japanese navy thus contributed significantly to the war operations of the Allied Powers, destroying armed German merchant cruisers in the Indian Ocean, attacking German submarines, and conducting sorties in European waters.

During the hostilities, Great Britain was gravely harassed by German U-boat operations, aimed at starving the British and forcing them to sue for peace. The situation had become so critical that the British Ambassador was constrained to write privately to Foreign Minister Motono, describing Britain's sad and difficult plight. The British Ambassador even requested the detailing of a Japanese fleet to Europe.

Meanwhile, in England, the Japanese Ambassador and Mrs. Chinda were hospitably received as honored guests of

King George and Queen Mary at Windsor Castle for two days, on which occasion the King personally requested the presence of a Japanese fleet in Europe. These earnest entreaties on Britain's part prompted the Japanese government to decide to reinforce its naval force in the European theater.

A year after Japan entered the First World War, she presented the famous "Twenty-One Demands" to China. It consisted of fourteen "demands" and seven "wishes," outlined in five groups, in which Japan demanded, among other things, the extension of the twenty-five year leases of Kwantung and of the South Manchuria Railway to ninety-nine years, the disposal of the German economic rights in Shantung, and, the transformation of the Han-Yeh-Ping Company which was supplying iron ore to Japan, into a Sino-Japanese joint enterprise.

Among Japan's "Twenty-One Demands," China evinced no serious objections towards the extension of the leases to 99 years and Japan's taking over of the former German rights in Shantung, but she did take strong exception to the "wishes" articles contained in Group V which pertained to the whole of China.

These articles of "wishes" consisted of such miscellaneous items as: the Chinese government to employ Japanese nationals as political, financial, and military advisers; to grant the right of land ownership in the interior of China to Japanese hospitals, temples, and schools; to permit Japan to build the Wuchang-Kiukiang-Nanchang, Nanchang-Hangchow, and Nanchang-Chaochow railways.

It should be noted here that the Western powers also entertained grave doubts about these articles of "wishes." The United States, in particular, vigorously protested to Japan on the grounds that they contradicted the principles of equal opportunity and the open door, threatening Chinese sovereignty. Japan was even denounced as an aggressor nation.

On the other hand, Sir Edward Grey, in defense of Japan, spoke well of Japan's moderate demands in his memoirs, claiming that "Japan's demands toward China were moderate when compared with those of the Western powers. If a powerful European nation had been similarly placed," he said, "the demands would have been more aggressive."

Kato Takaaki, who was then the Minister for Foreign Affairs, could by no means be described as an aggressive statesman. One of the overriding reasons for his determination to enter the war against Germany was his desire to obtain the extension of the leases on of Kwantung and the South Manchurian Railway.

Before taking up his new post as Foreign Minister, he met Sir Edward Grey in London in the hope of acquiring Britain's understanding on the issue of seeking an extension to the twenty-five year leases of the Leased Territory of Kwantung and the South Manchuria Railway, which were to expire soon after his return to Japan. He was anxious to have these leases extended to ninety-nine years, as were the cases of the Former German holdings of Tsingtao and Kiachow.

Kato also confided to Sir Edward Grey that the "Japanese have no intention of allowing Manchuria to pass out of their hands." To illustrate his point, he said the "Japanese, having planted the sapling in their garden, now happily awaited it to mature into a fine tree." Sir Edward personally encouraged Kato, adding that the "Japanese not only planted the tree, but watered it with their own blood." He, thus, implicitly recognized the validity of Japan's claim to extend the leases in Manchuria.

As stated earlier, Japan's main motive for becoming a

belligerent was to extend the leases of Port Arthur, Talien, and the South Manchuria Railway. But shortly after Japan entered the war, Great Britain was surprised to learn through Foreign Minister Kato that Japan, notwithstanding Britain's acquiescence to Japan's retention of Tsingtao after the German forces were driven out, would return Tsingtao to China. Great Britain, moreover, considered it quite natural that Japan should attach certain preconditions for restoring Tsingtao to China.

Foreign Minister Kato then summoned the Dutch Minister to clarify Japan's attitude toward Indonesia. When Kato pointed out that Japan entertained no ambitions in regard to Dutch possessions in Asia, the Dutch Minister joyously sprang to his feet. Noting the Dutch envoy's unconcealed relief, Kato inquired: "Had you been thinking that Japan would occupy Indonesia?" The Dutch Minister, while expressing profound words of gratitude, merely replied: "No, I had not been anticipating such an event." But before Kato could say anything further, the Dutch Minister had bolted from his presence.

This is further evidence that Japan had no aggressive intention in deciding to join the Allies in the war. Japan's sole aim was to find solutions to the pending problems of the day, in line with Japan's political and economic interests and in keeping with the prevailing international situation. In all my extensive reading of the innumerable official, diplomatic and authentic documents relating to the circumstances that led to Japan's participation in WWI, I have not found a scrap of evidence, aside from misleading and false propaganda, to support the claim that Japan's diplomacy was aggressive.

Meanwhile, with the progress of the war, Japan was placed in a difficult position as Britain, contrary to her initial policy of limiting Japan's operational zone only to the Far East, began to appeal for the urgent dispatch of the Japanese fleet to the Mediterranean Sea or to the Indian Ocean. In addition, Japan received pressing demands from France, Belgium, and even Great Britain to send an expeditionary force of about ten divisions of Japanese troops to the Western front. Foreign Minister Kato approved the request for the dispatch of some Japanese cruisers to the European war zone, but firmly rejected all requests for Japanese army divisions to be sent to Europe on the ground that Japan's armed forces existed for national defense and, therefore, could not be used for any other purpose.

In the meantime, as the military men began to wield greater influence in the political life of Japan, reactionary elements were quick to seize their opportunity, completely transforming Japan's foreign policy which had hitherto been formulated by the Gaimusho, the Ministry of Foreign Affairs. With General Terauchi at the helm of the Cabinet, Japan proclaimed her readiness to join the Siberian Expedition, originally proposed by the United States in order to rescue and repatriate the isolated remnants of the Czechoslovak army in Siberia.

The United States, however, was unable to calmly watch the situation in which the Japanese troops had continued to advance swiftly eastwards, until they had reached the halfway point in Siberia. Fearing that its action would constitute a serious subject of debate at the Washington Conference, Japan was obliged to proclaim the complete withdrawal of her troops. In the candid views of Takaaki there was no more meaningless and useless adventure comparable to the Siberian Expedition. Despite these developments, the moderate elements in the government and the Gaimusho were still able to control the high-handedness of the militarists. Their excesses, the few that did occur, at least were properly held in check by the government.

Versailles Peace Conference

WITH THE signing of the Armistice on November 11, 1918, World War I ended with the defeat of Germany. The formal Peace Conference of Versailles began on May 7 and the Treaty of Peace was signed on June 28, 1919. Under the terms of that treaty, earlier Japanese demands and basic interests were generally assured. The Marshall and the Caroline Islands, all German possessions in the Pacific Ocean north of the Equator which the Japanese navy had occupied during the war, were placed under the jurisdiction of Japan in accordance with the newly adopted mandate system of the League of Nations.

That Japan was able to get her demands accepted without any serious obstacle may be attributed to the fact that during the course of the war, Japan had participated in the London Declaration, an agreement which bound the participating powers not to enter into discussions of the peace terms. Moreover, at the time of the dispatch of her fleet to European waters, Japan had persuaded Great Britain and the other Allied Powers to acknowledge Japan's possession of the former German-held islands, the disposition of which, in Britain's view, should be postponed until after the war.

Japan also proposed the question of racial equality at the Race Conference, to which China, while opposed to Japan over the question of the disposition of the old German leased territory in Shantung Province, acted in concert. Japan's proposal was aimed at introducing a phrase in the preamble of the Covenant of the League of Nations which would endorse "the principle of the equality of nations and the just treatment of their nationals."

Woodrow Wilson, the American President, took a sympathetic attitude, as did the majority of the powers in support of the Japanese proposal, but the British colonies with so many different races, and particularly Australia, with its "White Australia Policy" led by Prime Minister Hughes, emphatically opposed the Japanese proposal. Thus, the draft of the Covenant of the League of Nations was adopted on April 28, 1919, without the provision of the racial equality for which Japan had so forcefully campaigned.

When I visited Brazil in 1961, I was informed that Japan's proposal to obliterate the color bar in international relations at the Peace Conference, has always formed an important principle in Brazil's fundamental foreign policy. The fact should not be overlooked that Japan's racial equality proposal undoubtedly had a greater impact on the various dependent races in Asia and Africa than can be imagined.

CHAPTER 14

Washington Conference

TAKING advantage of the expiration of the Third Anglo-Japanese Alliance in 1921, the United States took the initiative in summoning a historic conference—the so-called Washington Conference—which met in Washington, D.C. from November 11, 1921 until February, 1922.

Prior to this conference, the Japanese government had evinced a desire to renew the Anglo-Japanese Alliance to which Great Britain had raised no objection. Japan's position was that under the alliance she could expect Britain's assistance in the event she should be involved in some controversy against a third power and confronted by a situation in which, by virtue of the Allied victory, the Anglo-Saxon powers would be in a position of foremost influence. Should the pact be abolished, Japan feared that circumstances would compel Great Britain to station a powerful navy in the Far East. Japan, being racially different from the other leading powers of the world, might be exposed to anti-Japanese sentiments openly directed by foreign countries, once this alliance was terminated.

For these reasons, the Japanese government felt that it

71

would be wise to maintain friendly relations with a big power like Great Britain. In addition, Japan believed that the continuance of the Anglo-Japanese Alliance would help the cause of peace in the Far East, the maintenance of which Britain's Far Eastern policy regarded so essential for her economic interests. Japan felt also that Britain was satisfied with the status quo. Japan and Great Britain, however, thought it necessary, first of all, to bring their alliance in line with the covenant of the newly established League of Nations. Consequently, they submitted two joint notifications of the existence of the alliance to the League of Nations.

As stated earlier, while Great Britain had no objection to the continuance of the Anglo-Japanese Alliance, Canada vigorously opposed it. The main reason for the opposition was that, while the alliance had marked Germany as a potential enemy, with the elimination of the German and Russian threats, there was apprehension that the United States might assume the position vacated by Germany.

To the astonishment of Japan, Australia—led by Prime Minister Hughes, who had earlier energetically opposed the question of racial equality at the Versailles Peace Conference—turned around to support the maintenance of the alliance. Australia, then suffering from a general fall in commodity prices, had no other recourse but to pin her hopes, economically and politically, on the Anglo-Japanese Alliance in view of Britain's apparent inability to extend relief to Australia because of her own depressed business conditions at home. Australia also felt that she could place little reliance on Britain's weak naval base in Singapore.

It was in such a world situation that the Washington Conference was convened. Primarily due to American insistence at this conference, the Anglo-Japanese Alliance was finally abrogated. The position taken by the American government to press for the invalidation of the Anglo-Japanese Alliance was based on her misunderstanding that Japanese encroachments in Korea and Manchuria as well as moves toward China, were carried out with the backing of the said alliance.

In the place of this alliance there emerged the Four Power Treaty entered into by Japan, Great Britain, the United States and France for the maintenance of the status quo of the Pacific area. The four Power Treaty was followed by the Nine Power Treaty of February 1922, which concretely defined the principles of the open door and equal opportunity in matters concerning China. The signatories of the Nine Power Treaty were Japan, Great Britain, the United States, France, China, Italy, Belgium, the Netherlands, and Portugal.

Under the terms of this treaty, the powers concerned agreed to respect the sovereignty, independence, and territorial integrity of China; to provide the fullest and most unembarrassed opportunity to China to develop and maintain for herself an effective and stable government; to maintain the principles of equal opportunity for the commerce and industry of all nations throughout the territory of China; not to enter into any treaty, agreement, or understanding with China which would impair the principles of the open door and equal opportunity. China also for the first time agreed to respect the open door and specifically agreed that "she will not exercise or permit unfair discrimination of any kind" on her railways, while the other powers also assumed a similar obligation in respect to their railways in China.

The principle of equal opportunity was first enunciated in 1899 by John Hay, the then U.S. Secretary of State, in his famous circular note to all powers interested in the fate of China. The note clearly stated that all powers, within their spheres of influence, would preserve China as a territorial and administrative entity, and would not exercise unfair discrimination on customs duty, railway fares, and harbor improvement expenses. Later, the United States formulated the words "equal opportunity" in a larger scope from the original meaning expressed in the circular note, and this was clearly manifested in the negotiations on the question of Manchuria with Japan and Russia in the year preceding the war.

Ever since she proposed the Neutralization Plan for the Manchurian Railway, the United States—a late arrival on the China scene after the other powers had already staked their claims—endeavored to remove these spheres or influence and special interests from China under the banner of her "open door" policy.

Thus, the question of the open door was injected into the discussion at the Washington Conference when Charles Evans Hughes, the U.S. Secretary of State, presented a draft resolution for applying more effectively the principle of the open door or equal opportunity for the trade and industry of all nations in China. Consequently, the words "equal opportunity" with respect to China received a wider meaning and, at the same time, assumed a more binding international legal status in the Nine Power Treaty.

It should perhaps be pointed out here that even the meaning of the words "sphere of influence" is somewhat obscure, describing a power's special position pertaining to commercial or other vested interests in China. Wang Chunghui, Chinese delegate to the Washington Conference, explained in his speech at the conference that he believed Germany first made this assertion in relation to Shantung Province, but its exact origin has still to be traced.

Another agreement reached at the Washington Conference —the Naval Limitation Treaty of February, 1922—called for a sweeping reduction of naval armaments, stipulating the maximum capital ship tonnages at the ratio of 5–5–3–1.75 & 1.75, respectively for the United States, Great Britain, Japan, France, and Italy. An agreement on the limitation of the defense installations in the Pacific was also concluded.

At the time of the conference, Japan had an Eight-Eight Fleet Building Program, consisting of eight battleships and eight cruisers, some of which were already under construction, with the famed battleship "Mutsu" nearing completion. Great Britain, on the other hand, was also proceeding with the planned construction of four new super dreadnoughts of the Hood class. The United States, too, had a substantial tonnage of battleships and cruisers under construction or recently launched.

The agreement, limiting naval armaments, was concluded among the United States, Great Britain and Japan, envisaging the scrapping of the battleships in existence as well as those under construction, aggregating 1,876,000 tons. Japan at first insisted the ratio limiting maximum capital ship tonnage be on the basis of 10–10–6, but ultimately conceded to the 5–5–3 ratio on the condition that due consideration be paid to the question of limiting defense installations in the Pacific.

The conclusion of the Naval Limitation Treaty was a leading factor which greatly contributed to lasting peace in the Far East, enabled the war-impoverished nations to devote themselves assiduously to the tasks of rehabilitation, and freed them from the unbearable financial burdens that a naval armaments race would have entailed. The fact that the understandings concerning the Far East and the Pacific were reached in a series of agreements which were smoothly and peacefully concluded, demonstrated Japan's willingness to act in accordance with the tenets of a cooperative and a peace-loving nation.

CHAPTER 15

Haphazard Foreign Policy Since the Manchurian Incident

AFTER THE Washington Conference, the reins of Japan's policy towards China—faced with an increasing need for reorientation—were firmly in the hands of Kijuro Shidehara, Minister of Foreign Affairs during the years 1924–29. He faithfully guided the destiny of Japan's foreign policy towards China, undertaking to execute the purport of the conference agreement to the letter.

This re-orientation of Japan's China policy was prompted chiefly by economic necessity, to make the Far East safe for international trade. Popularly known as the "Shidehara Policy," the four principles as enunciated in the Diet on January 18, 1927, by Baron Shidehara, may be summarized as follows:

1. To respect the sovereignty and territorial integrity of China, and scrupulosuly avoid all interference in her domestic strife.

2. To promote solidarity and economic rapprochement between the two nations.

3. To entertain sympathetically and helpfully the just efforts for the realization of such aspirations.

4. To maintain an attitude of patience and toleration in the present situation of China, and, at the same time, to protect Japan's legitimate and essential rights and interests by all reasonable means at the disposal of the government.

Meanwhile, with the lapse of the Anglo-Japanese Alliance and the consequent weakening of Japan's international bonds, China began to take up an increasingly aggressive attitude. She not only openly boycotted Japanese goods, but also insisted on the recovery of her Manchurian interests. To counter this change in stand, the extreme elements among the Japanese militarists, especially in the Kwantung Army in Manchuria, took up an inflexible position against China, leading finally to the outbreak of the Manchurian Incident in 1931. This historic incident had far-reaching consequences for Japan, culminating in her withdrawal from the League of Nations and official notification that she would no longer be bound as a member of the League as of March 28, 1935.

Soon after the outbreak of the Manchurian Incident Japan was ostracized by the world, charged with having acted against the Nine Power Treaty, and even branded as an aggressor. However, the fact that China made no serious effort to check civil war and internal chaos and, furthermore, did nothing to create conditions in which various interests could be transferred to her by the powers concerned, was one of the main causes of discord.

While Japan, through diplomatic negotiations over a long period of years, accomplished her national objectives to revise the unequal treaties, to place her finances on a sound basis, and to amend the legal system as well as to consolidate her domestic affairs, no comparable steps were taken by China. P.H. Clyde, a noted American historian, in commenting on the Far Eastern situation after the Washington Conference, said: "There is no anxiety of the powers invading China, rather is there the danger posed by China, which is far from being an organized nation, threatening the powers' interests in China. The principles of the open door or equal opportunity could well be based on the assumption that China is a representative nation. Without this prerequisite, these principles could hardly be attained."

In the light of these circumstances, it would be unfair to denounce only Japan as being responsible for the events surrounding the Manchurian Incident. As the scope of the incident widened, the growing influence of the military clique in the government of Japan could no longer be held in check. Events in Manchuria entered a new phase with the inauguration in 1932 of the new state of "Manchukuo," or the "State of Manchuria."

Then, in July, 1937, the Lukowkiao Incident erupted when Japanese troops were attacked by elements of the Chinese army, and Japan was irretrievably bogged down in the so-called China Affair. At the same time, developments in the military sphere could no longer be contained. Prior to this incident, Japan had withdrawn from the London Naval Conference in 1936, signaling a parting of the ways between Japan and the Western democratic states, including Great Britain and the United States.

Meanwhile, in Europe, World War II had broken out in September, 1939, and the Tripartite Treaty was consummated between Japan, Germany and Italy in the following year. This was followed in April, 1941, by the signing of the Russo-Japanese Neutrality Pact. Two months after the conclusion of this pact, however, Germany was engaged in hostilities against Russia. On the other side of the world, the Japanese Army marched into the southern part of French Indo-China in July, 1941. Japanese-American relations rapidly deteriorated as America clamped an embargo on the export of oil to Japan. The climax came on December 8, 1941, when Japan took up arms against the United States and was drawn into the vortex of World War II.

The question now arises as to what was Japan's foreign policy in the strained circumstances of those days. It is, perhaps, no exaggeration to say that after the Manchurian Incident there was no foreign policy of the Japanese government in a real sense. Mr. Kamimura Shinichi, former Japanese Ambassador to Turkey, and Mr. Okazaki Katsuo, former Minister of Foreign Affairs, both men of high intellect and long experience in foreign affairs, hold the same opinion with regard to Japan's foreign policy.

In the words of Mr. Kamimura: "I believe that Japan had no foreign policy——in the actual sense of the term from the time of the Manchurian Incident onwards till the end of the occupation of Japan. Japan's paramount preoccupation until the termination of the war was to redress the excesses of the militarists and restrain them from going too far. Never have I wanted so much to appeal to the people for support and been so disappointed at their indifference. The impossibility of making appeals directly to the people was also terribly frustrating."

Mr. Okazaki speaks in a similar vein: "Japan, having no actual diplomacy since the Manchurian Incident, was only leading a hand-to-mouth existence, endeavoring to explain away to the countries concerned the outrages committed by the militarists. Japan had, of course, no diplomacy worthy of mention during the Pacific War. If we must say something about Japan's policy towards other nations, we can only describe it as having been aimed at maintaining neutral relations with Russia to ensure the security of Japan's northern frontiers, and adjusting her relations with the countries of Greater East Asia. Reflecting on the past, Japan was erroneously optimistic about her relations with Russia. Moreover, she was not only grossly ignorant of the stiffened attitude taken by the Soviet Union in the face of the blunt behavior of the Japanese militarists following the German advance on Moscow, but also of the fundamental communist policy of dealing a fatal blow wherever possible against the nations of the free world."

At any rate, it would appear to be meaningless to discuss the question of Japan's diplomacy during the period following the Manchurian Incident up to the end of the allied occupation of Japan, insofar as both of these experienced authorities in the field of foreign affairs, have unhesitatingly admitted that Japan had no foreign policy during the years in question.

In his analysis of the question of Japan's foreign policy in the postwar years, Mr. Okazaki has revealed that "under allied occupation, while all matters affecting external relations were administered by General Headquarters (GHQ) of the Allied Powers, there was no room for diplomatic initiative on the part of the Japanese government. The whole of the foreign liaison work of the Japanese government and the Foreign Office was limited exclusively to negotiations with GHQ. During the occupation period, the policy of the government was directed towards achieving the conclusion of the Peace Treaty and the restoration of Japan's independence at the earliest possible date."

CHAPTER 16

Termination of War and Majority Nation Peace Treaty

O N AUGUST 15, 1945, Japan accepted the Potsdam
Declaration, finally bringing the war to an end. The
conference held in Potsdam, near Berlin, between
July 17 and 25 and attended by the heads of state of the
Soviet Union, the United Kingdom, and the United States,
drafted the provisions of the Potsdam Declaration. Consti-
tuting the basic policy of the Allied Powers towards Japan,
it was published on July 25. The Allies demanded "the
unconditional surrender" of the entire Japanese armed forces
and "the occupation of Japan by the Allied Powers."

Having acceded to the Allies, Japan entered a new stage
of occupation under the Allied Powers. Being a defeated
and an occupied nation, she no longer had even a semblance
of a foreign policy that nominally had not existed since the
Manchurian Incident.

However, after World War II, the world became sharply
divided into two hostile armed camps, one of the West and
the other of the East, led by the United States and the
Soviet Union, respectively. The antagonism between the
two camps developed into a cold war. General Douglas
MacArthur, the Supreme Commander of the Allied Forces,

in order to satisfy the wishes of the Japanese nation for the early recovery of independence, endeavored to accelerate the early consummation of the Peace Treaty ever since the beginning of the Allied occupation.

But the cold war was an impediment that stood in his way, making the fulfilment of a comprehensive peace treaty —so deeply desired by Japan—an impossibility. In accordance with the international situation, the United States and Great Britain began pursuing from the summer of 1949, a policy of concluding a peace treaty with the majority of nations, which would exclude the communist countries, such as the Soviet Union, Poland, and Czechoslovakia. The peace treaty, based on the majority nation formula advocated by the free nations, was intended to assist the recovery of sovereignty by Japan, and to subsequently welcome her into their camp as a collaborator on an equal status in resisting the communist camp. There was, however, no indication as to when this majority nation formula could be formally agreed upon.

In the meantime, in the rapidly changing Far Eastern situation, a sensational development suddenly rocked the world. This was the proclamation of the establishment in Peking of the People's Republic of China in October, 1949, by the Chinese Communist Party, which had driven the Nationalist Chinese under Chiang Kai-shek from the mainland of China. Shortly thereafter, the Chinese communist regime and the Soviet Union entered into a closely bound alliance. Mao Tze-tung and Chou En-lai visited Moscow to sign a 30-year Treaty of Friendship, Alliance and Mutual Assistance in February, 1950, with Japan defined as their potential enemy. In June of the same year, within four months of the conclusion of the said treaty, the North Korean army, trained, equipped, and mastermined by the

Soviet Union, launched an armed attack against the Republic of Korea.

Thus, in a far corner of the Far East, the cold war finally exploded into a local hot war. For three years, until the armistice was signed on July 27, 1953, the United Nations Forces assisted by the South Korean army, were engaged in a modern large-scale war against the North Korean army and the Communist Chinese volunteers.

In the fall of 1950, as a direct consequence of the outbreak of the Korean War, the United States arrived at a firm decision that the time had obviously come to terminate the occupation and conclude the peace treaty with Japan. In order to cope with the international communism of the Soviet Union and Communist China, the United States keenly felt the necessity to revise her former occupation policy, grant independence to Japan, and strengthen Japan's economy.

In Japan, on the other hand, there was at the time, not a few in public opinion circles who still insisted upon an all-out peace which embraced the Soviet Union and Communist China. Captivated by the illusion of neutrality, they strenuously persisted in their view that non-alignment with either the Free World or the Communist Bloc was the only way to defend peace. But this stand only contributed to the prolongation of the occupation, and to the needless delay in Japan regaining independence.

Thus, Japan stood at the critical fork in the road that would decide whether she would choose majority nation peace or all-out peace. Her choice would also determine whether Japan would join the ranks of the free world as a collaborator contributing to freedom and peace, or whether she would patiently wait until the cold war antagonism which hampered the all-out peace had been dispelled. In view of the circumstances, it is quite natural that the then Liberal Party Cabinet under Prime Minister Yoshida chose the former course.

CHAPTER 17

Treaty of Peace · with Japan

I T IS THE LATE John Foster Dulles who unquestionably deserves the principal credit for having drafted the Treaty of Peace with Japan. In his dual role of adviser to the U.S. State Department and special envoy of President Harry S. Truman, Mr. Dulles, a Republican, finally succeeded in getting an agreement on the draft of the peace treaty after three separate visits to Japan and a hurried round of talks in the capitals of the leading Allied Powers.

This successful accomplishment was possible not only because of the special consideration shown by President Truman in appointing Mr. Dulles as a State Department adviser with the object of winning full congressional support, but also due to the firm belief and outstanding statesmanship of Mr. Dulles himself.

The objective of American policy was directed towards enlisting the cooperation of Japan to the side of the Free World in the cold war. Therefore, during the progress of the negotiations on the treaty, the United States earnestly sought the cooperation of the Allied Powers to make generous concessions on reparation and economic questions so as not to leave Japan in a seriously crippled condition.

Having accepted the heavy responsibilities, Mr. Dulles spent nearly a year in diplomatic talks with the major powers before he was finally successful in drafting the Treaty of Peace based on "amity and trust."

On September 4, 1951, the peace conference was summoned in San Francisco, attended by 52 nations including Japan, at which the Treaty of Peace with Japan was signed by 48 nations. Only the Soviet Union, Czechoslovakia, and Poland did not affix their signatures to the treaty. Having had her sovereignty fully restored by the Allied Powers, Japan was thus able to return to the international community of nations six years after the end of hostilities.

It should be noted here that China was omitted from the conference which also did not see the participation of India and Burma. However, shortly after the San Francisco Conference, Japan concluded separate treaties of peace with both India and China, and later with Burma.

With respect to China, Japan initiated negotiations on a separate treaty of peace in February, 1952, and signed the pact in April of the same year. The decision to exclude China from the Peace Conference in San Francisco was a compromise plan to enable Japan to have the right of choice between the People's Republic of China and Nationalist China in view of the fact that the United States recognized Nationalist China as the de jure government, while Great Britain recognized the People's Republic of China.

India's non-participation in the San Francisco Conference was motivated by friendly sentiments—on grounds that the treaty did not recognize Japan's position as honorable and equal. With India, Japan entered into a treaty of peace in June, 1952, and following prolonged negotiations, reached an agreement with Burma in November, 1954, on the questions of reparations and the peace treaty.

CHAPTER 18

San Francisco Formula

SIMULTANEOUSLY with the conclusion of the peace treaty with the United States, Japan signed the Japan-United States Mutual Security Treaty. By signing the peace treaty, although Japan freed herself from the occupation control of the Allied Powers, she delegated—under the terms of the Mutual Security Treaty—the responsibility for her defense to the United States forces stationed in and around Japan to "deter armed attack upon Japan." This arrangement is commonly known as the San Francisco Peace Treaty Formula.

However, there was a section of the public in Japan which deeply resented this San Francisco formula, claiming that Japan had lost her autonomy by authorizing United States forces to be stationed on her territory. Notwithstanding this opposition, having accepted the majority nation peace treaty as advocated by the United States and Britain, it was only natural for Japan to consider the question of her own security after recovering independence. The mutual security pact was, in fact, initiated and proposed by Japan.

The situation can best be clarified by quoting from the

book "The World and Japan," written by the then Prime Minister, Yoshida Shigeru. In the words of Mr. Yoshida:

"The Japanese proposal, in simple terms, was to establish a joint defense relationship between Japan and the United States, under which Japan would accept the stationing of United States armed forces within her territory. In reply to this proposal, the United States asserted that it could not, in light of Japan's inability to be on the basis of lasting and effective self-reliance and mutual assistance, agree to stipulate under a treaty the type of relationship desired by Japan. The United States, anxious that Japan should quickly regain such qualifications as a nation, agreed as a temporary measure to protect Japan by maintaining her forces in and around Japan."

Not only did Japan closely align herself with the United States and the free world by adopting the San Francisco formula, but by her decision to arrange for her own defense, Japan, at the same time, further strengthened the defensive position of the free world in the Far East.

It would be worthwhile to take a more thorough look at the important question of Far Eastern defense. American Secretary of State Dean G. Acheson declared in January, 1951, that the United States must be prepared to defend Japan militarily, not only for the security of the United States, but for Japan's own security. He went on to affirm that this line of defense extended from the Aleutian Islands to Japan and the Ryukyus down to the Philippine Islands.

Acheson's statement signified that the United States was applying the Truman Doctrine—the policy of containing the forces of communism—to the Far East, and the Japan-United States Security Treaty was nothing more than the extension of this policy. In other words, the treaty confirmed that an armed attack against Japan would be considered as an attack on the American line of defense in the Far East.

For a virtually defenseless Japan, the Japan-United States Security Treaty was absolutely indispensable, comparable in significance to Japanese diplomacy as the Anglo-Japanese Alliance in the Meiji Era.

CHAPTER 19

Admission of Japan
to the United Nations

IT WAS QUITE logical for Japan in making a fresh
start as a result of the San Francisco Peace Treaty, to
adopt the principles of the United Nations as one of the
cornerstones of Japanese foreign policy. In this connection,
let us take a look at the situation which prevailed prior to
Japan's admission to the world organization. The fact that
Japan was unable to gain entry into the world body without
serious difficulties is attributable to cold war influences.

Even earlier than the peace treaty, Japan had evinced
her wish to be admitted into the United Nations Organization. She applied to the Secretary General for membership
in June, 1952, two months after the treaty became operative.
The Japanese application was considered by the Security
Council in September. However, despite the voting of ten
to one in favor of Japan's admission, the Soviet Union by
resorting to the veto, was able to reject the application.

The reasons for the Soviet objection were: (1) the San
Francisco Peace Treaty did not provide any measures to
prevent the revival of an aggressive Japan; (2) Japan, under
the occupation of foreign forces, is not a sovereign state; (3)
a state of war still exists between Japan and two permanent

members of the Security Council (the Soviet Union and China) and, furthermore, by providing a military base for the American invasion of Korea, Japan cannot be regarded as a peace-loving state.

However, the Seventh General Assembly of the United Nations in December, 1952, adopted a resolution initiated by the United States which recognized Japan's qualification for membership, with 50 in favor, 6 (Soviet bloc countries) against, 4 abstentions and 1 absent.

At the following Eighth Session of the General Assembly, the Soviet representative, speaking in a perceptibly milder tone on the issue of Japan's membership, disclosed that the question was still premature as Japan had not yet concluded peace treaties with two of the five major powers. Nevertheless, he said, "an avenue will be open if Japan should conclude treaties of peace with the two powers concerned."

At the Ninth General Assembly in 1954, the delegates of the United States, India, Pakistan, Egypt, and Argentina unreservedly supported Japan's membership, emphasizing that it was only natural that she should be admitted to the United Nations. The representative of the Soviet Union, on the other hand, expressed a willingness to include Japan and other states supported by the Western powers in the list of 14 states which the Soviet Union proposed to collectively admit into the United Nations.

In the following year, 1955, the Tenth General Assembly adopted the plan to collectively admit 18 states, including Japan, but during the deliberations in the Security Council on the individual applications of the 18 states, the application of Mongolia was vetoed by Nationalist China. Thus, the move to admit 18 states en bloc proved abortive as the Soviet Union retaliated by exercising her veto power on the 13 non-communist countries listed for collective admission.

Under these circumstances, while collaborating with the United States, the Hatoyama Cabinet redoubled its efforts to improve relations with neighboring Asian countries, including Communist China and the Soviet Union. Negotiations to resume diplomatic relations were started with the Soviet Union.

In October, 1956, the two countries signed the Joint Declaration, terminating the state of war between them and restoring normal diplomatic relations. In the same declaration, the Soviet Union promised to support Japan's entry into the United Nations. In December, at the Eleventh General Assembly session, Japan's application was finally approved.

With the exception of two member nations that were absent—Hungary and South Africa—77 states attended the session in which the joint resolution for Japan's membership, sponsored by 51 Afro-Asian nations, was unanimously endorsed. Japan, thus, became the 80th member of the United Nations.

Less than a year later, in October, 1957, Japan, strongly backed by the United States and Britain, was elected by the Twelfth General Assembly to sit as a non-permanent member on the Security Council. Elected at the same time were Canada and Panama. Japan served a two-year term from January, 1958.

chapter 20

Revision of
the Security Treaty

WITH THE coming into effect of the peace treaty, Japan was able to resume her diplomatic activities. She could not, however, immediately pursue a strictly independent foreign policy. In other words, insofar as Japan was concerned, ever since the peace treaty went into operation, the San Francisco formula continued to contribute greatly towards maintaining her peace and security.

It should be recognized that the Japan-United States Security Treaty was signed at a time when the Far Eastern situation was tense and Japan possessed no adequate means of self-defense.

In the meantime, as the Korean War stalemated into a condition of cease-fire, Japan was able to gradually augment her defensive strength. The nation also began to show more awareness towards the question of national defense. To meet the exigencies of this changing situation, it was quite natural that the demand for the revision of the security treaty should grow more insistent.

The object of the revision was to place Japanese-American relations on the basis of mutual accommodation, that is, to transform the treaty from one of "United States being responsible for Japan's defense" into a defensive arrangement under which the defense of Japan would be "a joint undertaking of both Japan and the United States."

It must be frankly acknowledged that the original Japan-United States Security Treaty was characterized by unilateral responsibility, lacking any bilateral basis or equal-footing.

Among the vital issues requiring immediate attention were: (1) the United States, while permitted to station its armed forces on Japanese territory, was not obligated under the treaty to assist Japan in the event of an armed attack; (2) the United States was empowered to use her troops stationed in Japan for the maintenance of peace and security of the Far East, without prior consultation with Japan; (3) the United States forces in Japan could be employed, at the request of the Japanese government, to suppress any large-scale civil war or disturbances, and (4) among other things, the treaty made no mention of the period of validity, nor did it provide for any notification of abrogation.

In negotiating for the revision of the treaty, it was Japan's intention to correct these anomalies, conditions which appeared to suit only the requirements of the United States.

Shortly after the outbreak of the Korean conflict, in July, 1950, under a directive from General MacArthur, Japan's self-defense posture received its first positive impetus with the establishment of the National Police Reserve of 75,000 men to supplement the nation's police force to ensure national security. In August, 1952, with the inauguration of the Safety Agency, the National Police Reserve and the Maritime Safety Force were placed under the jurisdiction of the new agency and reorganized respectively as the National Safety Force and the 1,700-man Coast Guard Force.

Later in July, 1954, the Safety Agency expanded into the

Japan Defense Agency, adding an aviation wing to the National Safety and Coast Guard Forces. With this latest development, Japan's self-defense strength was increased to 152,000 men, comprising an integrated force of land, sea and air, united under the command of the Safety Agency.

Japan's subsequent request for a revision of the security treaty met with a negative response from the United States which expressed its readiness to enter into negotiations on the condition that Japan further increased her defense capability. To meet this condition, Prime Minister Kishi, who succeeded Hatoyama and Ishibashi at the helm of government, in February, 1957, drafted a long-term program for the modernization and improvement of the self-defense forces. After reaching a decision on implementing the first stage of the program covering a three-year period from 1958 to 1961, Prime Minister Kishi visited the United States in June as a preparatory step to the revision of the security pact.

During his official visit to Washington, Prime Minister Kishi met President Eisenhower and other high ranking administration officials in an effort to solve the pending questions between the two countries. The joint Japan-United States statement issued after these talks declared that "the President of the United States and the Prime Minister of Japan affirm that Japanese-American relationship, founded on solid foundations of common interest and mutual trust, is now entering a new age."

On this occasion, both Prime Minister Kishi and President Eisenhower, reaffirming their belief that the Japan-United States Security Treaty was of a provisional nature, agreed to set up a committee of the two governments to examine all problems related to the security treaty in keeping with the new age of Japanese-American relations. The establishment of this joint Japan-United States Committee to meet the needs and wishes of the peoples of both nations in the field of maintaining their security, opened the door to the negotiations for the revision of the security treaty.

Later in September, 1958, during their conversations in Washington, both Japanese Foreign Minister Fujiyama and Secretary of State Dulles, voicing their conviction that the Japan-United States Security Committee was intensifying the cooperation and understanding between the two nations, agreed to open talks for the revision of the treaty in Tokyo.

Although formal negotiations were started in October between Foreign Minister Fujiyama and American Ambassador MacArthur in Tokyo, it was not until January 6, 1960—after 15 months of intensive negotiations and 22 separate meetings—that the two sides arrived at a final agreement. The new Japan-United States Security Treaty was signed by Prime Minister Kishi Nobusuke and Secretary of State Christian Herter on behalf of their respective governments in Washington on January 19.

No other issue of public attention, national or international, had given rise to such confusion and uproar as did the question of revising the security pact. The difference of opinion between the opposing sides, one led by the government and the Liberal Democratic Party, and the other by the Socialist and Communist Parties, could hardly have varied more. Their respective positions on the treaty were 180 degrees apart, one side supporting the revision, the other demanding its abolition.

In a move to have the new treaty ratified by the National Diet, the government introduced it on the floor of the House on February 5, 1960, but the storm that ensued proved almost uncontrollable. While the treaty was being deliberated in the National Diet, massive and riotous demonstrators led by the National Council for Obstruction of the Revised Treaty, and the Zengakuren students' movement, surged around the parliamentary building for days. Despite these unprecedented demonstrations and stormy protests, the Liberal Democratic Party forcefully passed the revised treaty in the House of Representatives on May 20, and the new treaty became automatically operative thirty days later on June 20 without having been deliberated in the House of Councillors.

At a time when national feelings were at a high pitch, the opposition forces rallied their supporters in a move to prevent the scheduled visit of President Eisenhower to Japan to commemorate the 100th year of Japanese-American relations. A disgraceful incident occurred shortly after the arrival in Tokyo of Presidential Press Secretary Hagerty, who narrowly escaped by an American Marine Corps helicopter from the unruly mob that had encircled his car at the Haneda Airport. Faced with this grave situation, the government had no other alternative but to request the cancellation of President Eisenhower's projected visit to Japan, leaving behind an indelible stain on the history of Japanese-American relations.

chapter 21

Insertion of
the Economic Clause

THE MOST important revision contained in the new Japan-United States Security Treaty, according to the interpretation of Foreign Minister Fujiyama in the Diet, were as follows:

First, the treaty clearly stated that it was based on the principles and spirit of the United Nations.

Second, the treaty stipulated the obligations of the United States forces for the defense of Japan.

Third, the treaty gave Japan a voice in the operation of its provisions, such as the right of prior consultation in matters affecting the disposition of nuclear weapons into Japan and the movement of United States forces in Japan.

Fourth, the treaty added a new provision which called for the cooperative efforts of both Japan and the United States to promote their mutual relations in the political and economic fields.

Fifth, both nations agreed to exclude the clause pertaining to internal disturbances.

Sixth, after the treaty has been in force for ten years, either party may give notice of its intention to terminate the treaty, in which case it shall terminate one year later.

The fourth provision concerning economic cooperation was not actually in the first draft of the Foreign Ministry. On the other hand, the earlier Sino-Soviet Treaty of Alliance, the North Atlantic Treaty Organization, and the Southeast Asia Treaty Organization all contained stipulations for economic assistance and cooperation.

I referred to this absence of any mention of economic assistance in the Japan-United States Security Treaty of Prime Minister Kishi and Foreign Minister Fujiyama and strongly urged that such a clause be inserted into the treaty. At the same time, I solicited the support of other prominent personages in the political and economic circles.

The security treaty, essentially a military pact, actually originated as a result of the shock and fear created by the Sino-Soviet Treaty of Alliance and the Korean War which followed that alliance. The treaty, which has never been invoked since its inception, should not be called upon to exercise its provisions so long as there is no threat of aggression against Japan in the future.

Thus, in order for the Security treaty system to win the sympathetic support of the nation at large and to continue to function for an extended period, it is very important that the economic and political cooperation between the two countries be put into actual practice.

For example, in the case of NATO, Article 2 stipulates the encouragement of economic collaboration. American economic cooperation with Europe, which gave effect to Article 2 of the treaty, steadily strengthened belief that cooperation in the economic field was even more important in the maintenance of security than the strictly military element.

Expressed in other terms, NATO became a highly political alliance, operating in the belief that the political discussions, economic collaboration, development of resources, educational progress, and popular understanding among the peoples of the member countries were as important, if not more so, than the construction of warships or equipment of armed forces. The same thing may be said to apply in the case of SEATO.

Likewise, the new security treaty should also function not merely militarily but as a highly political alliance in the fields of politics, economics, and culture. The duration of such a treaty should be on a long term basis, operating with a comprehensive outlook.

Particularly in relation to economic collaboration, ever since the new line of "peaceful coexistence and competition" was enunciated by Soviet Premier Khrushchev, the questions of expanding trade and introducing foreign capital or technical cooperation, have gone beyond the purely economic stage and taken on political implications.

Fortunately, the new security treaty included in its preamble the desire of the two countries to increasingly promote economic cooperation and further the conditions of economic stability and welfare between them. Article 2, which stated that the two countries will "seek to eliminate conflict and encourage collaboration in their economic policies," was a newly added provision.

Moreover, on the occasion of the signing of the treaty, in the third paragraph of the joint communique of Prime Minister Kishi and President Eisenhower, the two leaders referred to the expansion of trade and assistance to underdeveloped countries. They summed up their views in these words: "The President fully concurred with the Prime Minister's view that it was extremely important that continuing discussions should be held on economic questions of mutual interest to Japan and the United States."

I am firmly convinced that the provisions of the treaty and the accompanying statement are essential to the prosperity of the Japanese economy, the stability of the Japanese people's livelihood, and Japan's venture to assist the less developed countries of the world.

CHAPTER

22

Validity of
the Security Treaty

I T SHOULD be added here that the validity of the Japan-
United States Security Treaty is limited to ten years,
terminating in 1970. Of course, as stipulated in Article
10 of the treaty, it will remain effective for as long as either
party fails to give notice to the other of its intention to terminate the treaty, but it shall become invalid one year after
such notice has been served. By terminating the treaty,
Japan will be neutralized, having broken her bonds with
the free world. At the same time, it is a matter of gravest
concern whether or not, by accepting neutrality, Japan will
have contributed to her own security.

Serious apprehension is felt in case the leftist elements,
which presently clamor for neutrality, should seize the reins
of government at the time the question of the security treaty's
renewal comes up for discussion. Judging from their past
actions, they will no doubt conduct an open movement for
Japan's neutrality. In this event, the Japanese people will
be faced with a critical decision as to whether they can
genuinely safeguard their own security by adopting a policy
of neutralization.

Supposing that, in such an event, Japan should become

neutral, it is not difficult to imagine either a direct Chinese Communist attack or, failing this extreme eventuality, Japan becoming a favorite target of massive pressure. By the year 1970, Communist China will have adequately equipped herself with limited nuclear arms and a delivery system, standing next only to the Soviet Union and the United States as a leading military power in the Far East. With its augmented fighting potential, Communist China will be able to exert military pressures against all the small neighboring states in the Far East.

The position of Japan is of great strategic significance. The loss of Japan, commanding the western end of the Pacific, will have far reaching consequences, crippling the sea supremacy currently held by the United States in the Pacific. Should a neutralized Japan ever succumb to Chinese Communist pressure, it is unlikely that the United States will stand idly by.

In any event, the neutralization of Japan will make the Far East situation extremely unstable. Hence, it is felt that the only path for Japan to pursue in the future is to continue the maintenance of the Japan-United States security system and, what is more important, to strengthen the structure of this system while, at the same time, avoiding any weakening of its effectiveness.

chapter 23

Jurisdiction of
the Northern Islands

D URING the Hatoyama administration, Japan and the
Soviet Union resumed diplomatic relations in accordance with the Japan-Soviet Joint Declaration signed
in Moscow on September 28, 1956. This declaration simply
stipulated that the islands of Habomai and Shikotan would
be restored to Japan when the two countries signed a peace
treaty. The final disposition of the northern territories was
left pending—territories that still continue under Russian
occupation since the end of the war.

Although it was not unexpected, the conclusion of the
new security treaty between Japan and the United States
promptly drew a sharp protest from the Soviet government.
The protest claimed that the new treaty would have serious
consequences on the various countries of the Far East and
the Pacific, not to speak of the Soviet Union and Communist China, which bordered on Japan. It went on to
charge that by voluntarily agreeing to the stationing of
foreign troops and the establishment of foreign military
bases, Japan was jeopardizing her own sovereignty and had
in effect surrendered her national independence.

Referring to the joint declaration in which the Soviet

Union had promised the return of the islands of Habomai and Shikotan to Japan upon the conclusion of the peace treaty, the Soviet Union stated that, in the light of the changed circumstances, she could no longer honor her pledges to return these islands until all foreign troops had evacuated from the territory of Japan.

The "territorial provisions" of the San Francisco Peace Treaty dealt very harshly with Japan. The country was compelled to renounce all her former overseas possessions, such as Korea, Taiwan, Kwantung Leased Territory, and the group of islands in the South Pacific under her mandate. Not only were the Chishima Islands and South Sakhalin wrested from Japan, but even territories considered an inherent part of Japan, such as the islands of the Amami group, the Ryukyu chain, and the Ogasawara Islands, were also placed outside her administrative jurisdiction.

Insofar as the southern islands and their relations with the United States were concerned, the American and British delegates in their declarations at the San Francisco Peace Treaty convention, recognized that Japan retained residual sovereignty over these islands. The question of Okinawa and Ogasawara (Bonins) will be dealt with in more detail in the following chapter. On December 24, 1953, the Amami group of islands was returned to Japanese sovereignty. Their restoration was welcomed as a Christmas gift from the then Secretary of State, Dulles.

With regard to the northern islands, Article 2, Chapter II, of the Treaty of Peace with Japan stated that "Japan renounces all right, title, and claim to the Kuril Islands, and to that portion of Sakhalin and the islands adjacent to it which Japan acquired as a consequence of the Treaty of Portsmouth of September 5, 1905." The treaty not only did not define the extent of the Chishima chain of islands, but laid down no stipulation as to the country which possessed it.

From the outset, Japan has always advocated that the Habomai and Shikotan islands were part and parcel of Hokkaido and did not belong to the northern islands, that is, the Kurils. Mr. Dulles made special reference to these islands at the San Francisco Conference, affirming that the United States view was identical to that of Japan.

Japan also maintained that Kunashiri and Etorofu islands were an integral part of the territory of Japan proper, and not a segment of the Kurils which Japan had renounced. Judging from the fact that Mr. Dulles made not the slightest allusion to the matter concerning these islands at the time of the San Francisco Conference, it appears that the United States government had not yet crystallized its views on the question.

When the Hatoyama Cabinet began negotiating with the Soviet Union, Foreign Minister Shigemitsu made it unmistakably clear to the Soviet government that Japan regarded Kunashiri and Etorofu as part of the territory of Japan proper, and that under the principles of the North Atlantic Charter and the Cairo Declaration which renounced territorial expansion, these islands should not be transferred to the Soviet Union.

After examining the question, the United States also confirmed the justice of Japan's stand. In a memorandum issued in September, 1956, Secretary of State Dulles asserted that both Kunashiri and Etorofu were islands that were under the sovereignty of Japan. There is no ground for argument that the issue of the northern islands, particularly Kunashiri and Etorofu, is an outstanding international question.

The San Francisco Peace Treaty, in reference to the

Chishima Islands, uses the definition "Kuril Islands." In Russian, the word "Kuril" denotes smoke, a definition which no doubt refers to the volcanic islands. The fact that Kunashiri and Etorofu do not belong to the Kuril chain is evident in treaties concluded in the distant past.

More than 110 years ago, in February, 1855, a Treaty of Friendship with Russia was concluded at the Chorakuji Temple in Shimoda, Izu, following negotiations between Kawaji Toshiakira and Admiral Poutiatine, representatives of the Tokugawa Shogunate and the Russian government, respectively. This treaty clearly defined the territorial limits of both countries, acknowledging that Kunashiri, Etorofu, Habomai, and Shikotan were part of Japan proper, and that the Kurils north of Urup Island were under Russian sovereignty. As for Sakhalin, it was agreed not to define its border line but to continue to apply the customary practices.

Nearly twenty years later, in 1874, Enomoto Buyo went to St. Petersburg to sign a treaty with the Russian government, exchanging Sakhalin Island for the Chishima Islands or the Kurils. Article 2 of the Treaty exchanging Sakhalin for the Chishimas stipulates that the Kuril Islands extend north of Urup Island to Shimshu Island, or a chain of 18 islands.

Since the San Francisco Treaty translated the Chishima Islands into the Kuril Islands, it goes without saying that this group of islands does not include Habomai, Shikotan, Kunashiri and Etorofu. These islands which have been Japanese possessions for such a long time may be aptly described as ancestral birthplaces of the Japanese.

As was previously stated, the Japanese-Soviet Joint Declaration restoring diplomatic relations between the two countries also agreed that there should be continuing negotiations for the conclusion of a peace treaty. In such negotiations for a peace treaty, it is a foregone conclusion that the question of the disposition of the Northern Islands should figure prominently in the parleys.

Later in August, 1961, when the Soviet First Deputy Mikoyan visited Japan, he handed a personal message from Premier Khrushchev to Prime Minister Ikeda, urging that Japan and the Soviet Union establish peaceful and friendly relations based on the principle of non-interference in each other's domestic affairs. In reply to this message, Prime Minister Ikeda reiterated Japan's stand that the return of Japan's territories is a prerequisite to any conclusion of a peace treaty between the two countries.

This communication was followed by further exchanges of correspondence between Premier Khrushchev and Prime Minister Ikeda on the question of territories, in particular the interpretation of Chishima Islands—two letters from Premier Khrushchev and one from Prime Minister Ikeda between September and December. In his message, Premier Khrushchev curtly retorted that all territorial questions have already been settled through a series of international agreements, that Japan had renounced her claims to Chishima and Sakhalin under the San Francisco Treaty, and it was strange for her to be talking about territories that she no longer possessed. Furthermore, continued Khrushchev, the Yalta Agreement did not divide Chishima into north and south but dealt with the problem of the Kurils as a whole.

In his rebuttal, Prime Minister Ikeda agreed that Japan had renounced its claims to Chishima and Sakhalin, but it had at no time declared that it would deliver these islands to Mr. Khrushchev as gifts. Stressing that Japan was not bound by the terms of the Yalta Agreement, he repeated that the Chishima Islands renounced under the San Francisco treaty included only the islands north of Urup, and did not embrace Kunashiri and Etorofu which are an integral part of Japan proper.

Expressing its views on the controversy over the northern territories between Japan and the Soviet Union, the United States State Department in December, issued a statement supporting Japan's claim as factual and legally justified.

Countries most directly involved in the issue of the territorial settlement of the northern islands include Japan, the Soviet Union, and the United States. It is, therefore, unlikely that the other Allied Powers will protest against any interpretation or solution which these countries may reach. The views of Japan and the United States fortunately are in agreement.

In dealing with the Soviet Union, there is no other course open but for the Japanese government, people, and political parties of all shades of opinion to unite, firmly advocating what has to be advocated, patiently and persistently until the justice of their cause is recognized by the only dissenting nation.

CHAPTER 24

Jurisdiction of
the Southern Islands

JAPAN'S unsettled territorial claims include not only the northern islands, but also the Ryukyu Islands and the Ogasawara or Bonin Islands to the south. With respect to the latter islands, Japan pledged in Article 3, Chapter II of the Treaty of Peace that "Japan will concur in any proposal of the United States to the United Nations to place under its trusteeship system, with the United States as the sole administrating authority—the Ryukyu Islands and the Bonin Islands—" and acknowledged in the said Article that "pending the making of such a proposal and affirmative action thereon, the United States will have the right to exercise all and any powers of administration, legislation, and jurisdiction over the territory and inhabitants of these islands, including their territorial waters."

By this article, the United States has the right to place these islands under trusteeship, with the United States as the sole administrating authority exercising the actual powers of administration until the realization of the trusteeship system. In other words, complete sovereignty did not rest with the United States but, as proclaimed at the San

Francisco Conference, she recognized the retention of "residual sovereignty" over these islands by Japan.

What is actually meant by "residual sovereignty" has never been clearly defined by international law. The popular conception of "residual sovereignty" associated the term to China's titular sovereignty over the leased territories of the Western Powers and Japan, as well as Turkey's formal sovereignty over Bosnia-Herzegovina which were mandated territories of the Austro-Hungarian Empire.

Residual sovereignty may, therefore, be interpreted as recognition by the country administering a territory, that it does not intend to remain permanently in power, and that its control will ultimately cease functioning.

Accordingly, United States recognition of residual sovereignty implied that it eventually intended to restore these territories to Japan. Needless to say, the effort of the United States to retain Okinawa and Ogasawara islands as a United Nations trusteeship, is based on ensuring security while coping with the tensions and threats in the Far East.

Fully realizing that it would be difficult to place these islands under United Nations mandate, the United States in provisionally administering these islands until they can be restored to Japan.

At the same time, Japan, which strongly desires the return of these islands, has never lost an opportunity to demand the restoration of Japanese sovereignty. The United States, on the other hand, has gradually been adopting a more lenient policy towards the islands under her jurisdiction.

Regarding Okinawa, the memory of the bloody sacrifices paid by the soldiers and civilians on the island during the closing days of the Pacific War, is deeply imbedded in the nation's memory. When the American forces occupied

Okinawa in April, 1945, Japanese soldiers who fell in action totalled 92,000, and a further 97,000 civilians died while assisting in the defense of the island stronghold.

The United States has continued to remain in military occupation of the island even after the end of the war and the signing of the peace treaty. This special situation of the island of Okinawa poses a crucial problem. While it is admitted and appreciated that the special position of Okinawa is largely due to strategic and defensive requirements, there is a point which should be emphasized, namely, that not only is Okinawa a vital link in the Japanese-American security system, but its strategic location is heightened by the fact that the United States also has separate mutual defense treaties with Korea, Nationalist China, and the Philippines. In addition, the base is of indirect importance to SEATO, the Southeast Asia Treaty Organization, and to ANZUS, mutual defense treaty among the United States, Australia, and New Zealand.

A noteworthy highlight in the negotiations between Japan and the United States over the problem of Okinawa, was the joint statement issued by Prime Minister Kishi and President Eisenhower during the former's visit to the United States in June, 1957. In this statement, Japan voiced her strong desire to have the administrative rights over Okinawa and Ogasawara returned, while the United States reaffirmed that Japan possessed residual sovereignty over these territories. Furthermore, the United States promised to enhance the welfare of the people of these territories and to continue making economic and cultural advancements.

Later, during the visit of Prime Minister Ikeda to the United States in June, 1961, a joint statement issued on the occasion by the Prime Minister and President Kennedy stated that the two leaders discussed various matters related to Okinawa and Ogasawara, during which the United States promised to make increased efforts to improve the tranquillity and welfare of the people of Okinawa. In this connection, it welcomed Japan's cooperation. Japan assured the United States of her continuing collaboration.

This marked increase in collaboration between the two countries was hailed as signalling a new stage in the development of Okinawa. The United States not only permitted the displaying of the Japanese flag in Okinawa but also agreed to Japanese assistance in the educational field. Reforms in labor laws were legislated and the two countries augmented their economic aid to the islands.

In March, 1962, President Kennedy issued an executive order aimed at reforming the administration of the Ryukyu Islands. In a related statement, President Kennedy clearly recognized the Ryukyus to be a part of the Japanese homeland. The United States government, he said, looks forward to the day when the security interests of the Free World will permit their restoration to full Japanese sovereignty.

To give expression to this policy, and in order to discharge more effectively their responsibilities to the people of the Ryukyus by minimizing the difficulties that will accompany the anticipated eventual restoration of the Ryukyus to Japanese administration, President Kennedy directed that the following specific actions be taken:

1. The appointment of a civilian administrator.
2. The nomination of the Chief Executive of the Government of the Ryukyus by the Legislature.
3. Asking Congress to amend the Price Act so as to remove the present ceiling on assistance to the Ryukyu Islands.
4. Entering into discussion with the government of Japan with a view to working out precise arrangements to implement a cooperative relationship between the United States and Japan in providing assistance to pro-

mote the welfare and well-being of the inhabitants of the Ryukyu Islands and their economic development.

In accordance with the new policy enunciated in this statement, President Kennedy, in March, 1962, appointed Shannon B. B. McCune to be civil administrator charged with the performance of such duties as may be assigned to him by Paul W. Caraway, then High Commissioner. In December, the Ryukyu Legislature was convened in an extraordinary session to nominate the chief executive. The incumbent chief executive, Seisaku Ohta, who was returned to office by the Legislature under the new nomination system, was appointed Chief of the Government of the Ryukyu Islands by the High Commissioner.

Moreover, the United States relaxed some of the restrictions that had been placed on personal liberties, and drafted a five-year plan for the development of the Ryukyus. The United States government followed up these initiatives by presenting a bill of $25,000,000 for assistance to the Ryukyu Islands, hitherto restricted to $6,000,000, a ceiling placed by the Price Act, but this amount was cut to $12,000,000 in the Senate and further reduced to $8,900,000 as assistance for 1963. Consequently, the implementation of the five-year development plan became practically impossible for fiscal 1963.

To give effect to the cooperative relationship between Japan and the United States, talks were held between Foreign Minister Ohira and Ambassador Reischauer in November, 1962. The two countries agreed to establish the Japan-United States Consultative Committee in Tokyo to discuss the question of assistance to the Ryukyus and, at the same time, to set up in Naha the Japan-United States Technical Committee, made up of members from Japan, the United States, and the Ryukyus, for the purpose of exchanging views on the practical implementation of the economic assistance. The establishment of these consultative bodies was timely, and it is rather surprising that their creation had been so long delayed.

However, the negotiations between Japan and the United States for the formation of these bodies subsequently continued for a year and a half without reaching a satisfactory conclusion, due mainly to the fact that Japan desired to enlarge the scope of the consultative organ by making it competent to deal with political problems as well—as a first step towards the restoration of the administrative rights to Japan—whereas the United States sought to limit the functions of the bodies only to economic issues.

Another factor contributing to the delay could well have been the fact that the High Commissioner was a military man, and the issues connected with the establishment of the two bodies had to be examined by not only the U.S. State Department, but also by the Department of Defense and the Ryukyu Civil Administration.

The indefinite attitude of the United States was also attributed to the critical developments related to Taiwan, following France's recognition of Communist China, and the generally deteriorating situation in Southeast Asia which profoundly increased the strategic importance of the Ryukyu base. On the other hand, with the increased capabilities of mass transoceanic movement of troops, development of long range missiles, and disposition of Polaris submarines, the time for re-evaluating the military bases had also arrived.

In the midst of these difficult negotiations, a most lamentable incident occurred on March 24, 1964 involving the stabbing of Ambassador Reischauer, who had been an earnest supporter of these consultative organs, by a mentally deranged Japanese youth. It is highly regrettable that the Ambassador's wound was serious enough to require prolonged medical attention and recuperation.

Having agreed to the principle, the Japanese government felt that the organs should be set up as quicky as possible. Formal negotiations were resumed in early April, and on the 25th, the creation of the two committees was, at long last, finalized.

The Ogasawara or Bonin Islands, according to the 1940 national census, were populated by 7,361 inhabitants comprising 1,334 households, but with the unfavorable tide of the war in 1944, they were forcefully evacuated to the main island by the military authorities. In the immediate postwar period, the American occupation authorities sanctioned in October, 1946, only the return of 135 persons of mixed blood with naturalized European ancestral origin. Even after the peace treaty became operative, the ordinary inhabitants of the islands were not allowed to return and are still unable to visit their ancestral graves.

The Japanese government has taken every opportunity to negotiate with the American authorities not only for the return of the Bonins, but also to allow the islanders to return to their native homes. While it is not difficult to understand that the United States wishes to retain control of the islands for military reasons, it is hard to believe that, in contrast to Iwo Jima, every island in the group has vital military installations. However, if the return of the former islanders cannot be sanctioned for the sake of military security, then there is, of course, no other alternative but to wait a while longer for the opportune moment when such military necessity preventing their return will cease to exist.

Tacitly acknowledging that there were no immediate prospects in sight for an early settlement of the Bonin Island issue, the Japanese government presented a proposal to the United States, seeking compensation for the losses sustained by the islanders owing to the U.S. government's action in barring their return to the islands. At first, the United States government appeared reluctant to entertain the proposal, but the compensation bill was finally passed in both the House of Representatives and the Senate in August, 1960, granting a solatium of $6,000,000. With the disbursement of this payment in June, 1961, the problem of compensation was finally settled.

The Amami Islands, as was stated earlier, were returned to Japan in December, 1953.

chapter 25

Normalization of
Japan-Korea Relations

WHILE the greater part of Japan's diplomatic issues was settled in the postwar years, the important questions of normalizing relations between Japan and Korea, and Japan and Communist China still awaited settlement. The relations between Japan and Korea, a country tragically divided into south and north at 38 degrees North Latitude, have not yet been normalized, despite prolonged negotiations conducted off and on during the past 12 years. There have lately been signs that the negotiations with South Korea are at last making positive progress, and that the long pending questions between the two countries will shortly be resolved.

Korea, under Japan's tutelage for 35 years until the end of the war, has inseparably close geographical, historical, cultural, and social ties with Japan. Both Korea and Japan are in the forefront of the free nations of the Far East, and the normalization of their relations is a prerequisite for their mutual security as well as for the stabilization and elevation of the livelihood of the peoples of the two countries. It is indeed strange that South Korea, which has already been recognized by 73 free nations of the world, should remain diplomatically aloof from Japan, a country separated from Korea by only a narrow strip of water. On the other hand, North Korea is recognized only by 19 countries, principally belonging to the communist bloc.

The 38th parallel originally marked the border which the United States and the Soviet Union agreed would divide their respective zones of occupation at the end of the last war. At the Foreign Ministers' Conference held in Moscow in December, 1945, the representatives of the United States, Britain, China, and the Soviet Union—respectively James Byrnes, Ernest Bevan, Wang Chih-chieh, and Vyacheslav M. Molotov—concurred that the four powers should administer Korea under a trusteeship within five years. In accordance with this agreement, a joint U.S.-U.S.S.R. conference opened in March, 1946, to discuss the establishment of a Korean provisional government.

However, the Soviet Union demanded that only those parties and organizations supporting the decisions of the Moscow Conference should be allowed to participate in the provisional government, and that rightist elements opposing the trusteeship should be excluded. The United States, on the other hand, opposed the Soviet stand on the ground that it infringed upon the freedom of expression. With the collapse of the conference, the United States referred the matter of the unification of Korea to the United Nations General Assembly in September.

In November, 1947, the United Nations General Assembly adopted a resolution calling for the holding of general elections throughout the whole of Korea under the supervision of the United Nations, and the establishment of a unified government. General elections were subsequently held only in the southern half of Korea and the Government of the Republic of Korea was formed in Seoul in August with Dr. Syngman Rhee as the nation's first President. In the north, a separate government of the Korean People's Democratic Republic was established in Pyongyang under Kimil Sung.

The United Nations, in adopting another resolution on the question of Korea, in December, 1948, affirmed that the government of the Republic of Korea was the only legal government of Korea. Following this decision, the United Nations permitted the Republic of Korea to dispatch an observer to the world forum.

In spite of these circumstances, a section of public opinion in Japan continues to maintain that the normalization of relations with South Korea would deepen the division existing between North and South Korea, jeopardizing the peace of Asia. The Socialist Party, for instance, advocates that formal diplomatic relations should be established only after the unification of the two parts of the country. Needless to say, Japan, which recognized the independence of Korea under Article 2 of the San Francisco Peace Treaty, ardently hopes that the unification of North and South Korea, so strongly desired by the Korean people, will be achieved in the shortest possible time.

With only the Republic of Korea accepting the United Nations formula for unification, and North Korea adamantly opposed to any United Nations mediation, it is difficult to foresee when unification will actually be achieved. Nevertheless, in view of various outstanding problems, particularly fisheries, it is intolerable that relations between Japan and Korea should remain in their present state of abnormality.

This state of affairs adversely affects the interests of the free nations of East Asia, allowing communist influences to drive a wedge between Japan and Korea. The memories of the Korean War, which dragged on for three years after the armed attack against the Republic of Korea by the North

Korean forces, heavily assisted by Communist China, cannot be easily forgotten. At the height of the war, the United Nations and South Korean forces were temporarily forced to retreat to the southern extremity of the Korean Peninsula, near the Pusan perimeter. There were even fears at one time that they might be driven into the Straits of Korea.

Late in July, 1961, North Korea, entering into Treaties of Friendship, Cooperation and Mutual Assistance with both the Soviet Union and Communist China, aimed its military alliances against the United States and Japan, aggravating still further any chance of unification between the two halves of Korea.

In view of these circumstances, it is reasonable for the free world to expect Japan to shoulder the obligation of normalizing her relations with the Republic of Korea in order to contribute to the latter's stability, and to the strengthening of peace in Asia. The frantic communist charge that Japan is attempting to link the Republic of Korea and the Nationalist government on Taiwan, with United States backing, into a NEATO (North East Asia Treaty Organization) pact, is not only evasive, but puerile, to say the least.

At the same time, a certain section of Japanese opinion is clamoring that the present administration in South Korea being a military and undemocratic regime set up after a coup d'etat, is not a proper party with which to hold negotiations. This argument holds little water, there being many diplomatically recognized regimes in the world which were established as a result of coups and other undemocratic processes, the Soviet Union and Communist China not excluded. The fact should not be overlooked that a presidential election was held in the Republic of Korea in October, 1963. A stable government was established by the

Democratic Republican Party which won 110 seats out of 175.

The military administration transferred governmental powers to civilian control in accordance with an earlier promise. That both the presidential and parliamentary elections were held in a free and fair atmosphere has been confirmed in a report by the United Nations Commission for the Unification and Rehabilitation of Korea. Hence, the denunciation just mentioned is without any foundation in fact. To enter into relations with a government which has been democratically elected is a matter of international practice.

Negotiations to normalize Japan-Korea relations began in October, 1951, with the first formal conference taking place on February 15, 1952. At the outset of the negotiations, both governments had hoped that the various outstanding problems between them would be largely settled before the anticipated signing of the San Francisco Peace Treaty in April, 1952, and that a basic treaty restoring diplomatic ties between the two countries would at least be agreed upon to coincide with the effectuation of the Treaty of Peace.

Before formal negotiations had a chance to get underway, President Syngman Rhee suddenly promulgated on January 19, 1952, his "proclamation of maritime sovereignty," unilaterally setting up the Rhee Line, or so-called Peace Line. The Korean President, contending that this line was necessary for national defense, included within its confines the Island of Takeshima attached to Shimane Prefecture to the east, the center of the Yellow Sea to the west, and the waters beyond the MacArthur Line (restricted by GHQ to navigation by Japanese ships) in closer proximity to Japan to the south.

This vast area, closed to Japanese fishing vessels, was

declared an area in which national sovereignty would be exercised for the protection of marine resources. The Japanese government vigorously protested against this illegal act of arbitrarily extending Korean territorial waters in defiance of international law.

The main subjects of the agenda of the Japan-Korea talks beginning on February 15 were the question of property claims as stipulated in Article 4 of the San Francisco Peace Treaty, the question of nullifying the Peace Line and concluding a fisheries agreement, and the question of the legal status of Korean residents in Japan. It was not surprising, however, that the Korean government's insistence on maintaining the Peace Line ruptured the negotiations.

Although the second talks were held in 1953, followed by the second and third conferences, and the fourth in 1958 after a five year suspension, the anti-Japanese policy of President Syngman Rhee killed any prospects of a speedy conclusion of the long drawn-out talks. During this period, the Korean government indiscriminately captured Japanese fishing vessels, detained their crews as "hostages," and persistently exerted pressures on Japan to extract concessions. While the repatriation of North Koreans further complicated the progress of the negotiations, Japan and Korea did come to an agreement in December, 1957, on the exchange of Japanese fishermen detained in the Pusan Camp and the illegal Korean entrants detained at the Omura Camp.

The April Revolution, in which the masses in South Korea demonstrated against dictatorial rule, swept President Syngman Rhee out of office after he had just been elected for a fourth term in March, 1960. With revived hopes, the fifth round of preliminary conferences opened in October with Rhee's successor, Premier Chang Myon. These talks were suspended in May of the following year due to a military coup d'etat.

The new military regime headed by Lt. General Chang Do Yong, Chairman of the Supreme Council for National Reconstruction, began instituting a program of national reconstruction. It also announced that one of the main external tasks would be to settle differences between Korea and Japan, leading to the establishment of diplomatic ties between the two nations. Before anything positive could be achieved, the power struggle within the Supreme Council finally forced the resignation of Chairman Chang. With the coming into power of General Park Chung Hee, the real strong man behind the coup, the military administration passed into firmer hands. In October, the preliminary talks leading to the sixth round of negotiations were opened between Sugi Michisuke, representing Japan, and Pe Ui Hwan, representing the Republic of Korea.

In Korea there were signs that public opinion was swinging in favor of an early restoration of relations between the two countries, stemming in part from the realization that collaboration with Japan was the best means of overcoming the economic crisis which was hampering Korean reconstruction. In November, 1961, Chairman Park, while en route to the United States, visited Japan, at which time he conferred with Prime Minister Ikeda. On the question of property claims, the two leaders agreed that the claims were not of a nature of reparations but were based on legal grounds. A further series of talks on property claims was held in 1961, resulting in November in a general understanding between Japanese Foreign Minister Ohira Masayoshi and Director of the Korean Central Intelligence Agency, Kim Chong Pil, that Japan would give Korea an outright grant of $300 million, extend $200 million as a long-term low interest loan, and provide an additional amount of more than $100 million in the form of a civilian cooperative fund.

Internal strife within the ruling military junta in Korea continued into 1963, culminating in the resignation and departure overseas of Kim Chong Pil, and the extension and subsequent cancellation of the military rule of Chairman Park. Faced with such a fluid state of affairs in Korea, Foreign Minister Ohira finally had to abandon any further serious attempt to reach a settlement.

With the presidential elections and the national assembly elections in the autumn of 1963, and the restoration of the Park Chung Hee-Kim Chong Pil line, conditions within the country returned to normal. The Japan-Korea negotiations which were resumed in January, 1964, took place under more promising prospects.

Following the restoration of political stability, the Korean government was immediately faced with the crucial problems of economic construction and stabilization. The poor harvest, failure of currency reforms, and graft had all but halted the progress of the five-year economic plan launched in 1962. The situation was also aggravated by America's policy to protect the dollar, leading to the trend to reduce overseas economic assistance. In these circumstances, the Korean government began turning its attention towards Japan, hoping that the restoration of diplomatic ties would lead to economic cooperation and assistance. It is not difficult to understand why President Park—more than anyone else—should be so keen to come to an early settlement with Japan.

The current Japan-Korea negotiations are centered on the question of fisheries. At the beginning of these talks the sharpest differences arose between Korea's efforts to establish a vast restricted area as exclusive fishing grounds, and Japan's attempts to narrow the width of the grounds and establish a joint restricted area along its outer border. Although the Korean government, as a concession, reduced the Rhee Line to a line extending for a distance of 40 nautical miles, the Japanese government could not agree to a point beyond 12 nautical miles as recognized by international law. The Korean side then agreed to consider the Japanese plan for the joint restricted area, but differences arose over the formula of drawing the base line for the exclusive fishing grounds.

In other words, in drawing the base line the Japanese negotiators insisted that the line should be drawn on the basis of the low tide line from the shore in accordance with international practice, whereas the Korean side asserted that it should be drawn in a straight line from the various large and small islands off the Korean Peninsula. Consequently, there was a wide disparity in the interpretation of the 12-nautical mile line. The acceptance of the Korean interpretation would bar Japanese fishing boats from the main fishing grounds around Cheju Island.

While it was agreed that the joint restricted area would in principle be 28 nautical miles, the Japanese and Korean drafts differed widely on the method and scope of restricting the areas around Tsushima Island. There was a sizable difference regarding the member of Japanese fishing vessels that would be allowed to operate in the joint restricted area. In addition, the Korean draft envisaged the establishment of a large prohibited fishing zone during the winter season south of the Rhee Line. Opinion also varied as to the conditions under which the $30 million would be extended as fishery cooperative funds.

On the other hand, the thorny question of fisheries finally passed from the administrative stage in March, 1964, to the ministerial level between the Ministers of Agriculture of the two nations, Akagi and Won. Had the Japan-Korea talks shown prospects of agreement, the Japanese government would have been willing to extend the parliamentary session beyond May 10, 1964, in order to have the treaty ratified. But, as Chief Cabinet Secretary Kurogane declared at the time, the student demonstrations in Korea had again dimmed any such prospects. Immediate normalization of Japanese-Korean relations had again receded.

On the issue of compensation, the Korean side had earlier submitted an eight-article demand, including payment for all gold and silver bullion removed from the Bank of Korea, and remuneration to Korean laborers drafted by Japan. It was later agreed that this right to claim compensation would be based on legal grounds, but the interpretation of legality differed between the two sides.

Owing to the confusion in the postwar years and the devastation caused by the Korean War, it was exceedingly difficult to ascertain facts, particularly since so many years had already elapsed. However, it would be deeply regrettable if differences over minor points should stand in the way of settling the more important problem of reaching an early agreement on normalizing relations.

In the greater interests of both nations and in consideration of their special past relationship, the Japanese government in successive talks with Korea decided to extend substantial credits and grants which would contribute to the stabilization of the Korean people's livelihood, and their economic development. An understanding had also been reached between the two nations on the extent of these payments and economic assistance.

Still to be settled is the question of how repayment is to be made on the credit, with Japan asking for repayment within thirteen years and Korea demanding that the period be extended to twenty years. On the question of redeeming the frozen securities, Korea is also demanding the extension of the period beyond that desired by Japan. But these are relatively minor issues.

Concerning the question of the legal status of 600,000 Koreans residing in Japan, agreement on general principles has already been reached.

Simultaneously with the coming into effect of the San Francisco Peace Treaty, which recognized the independence of Korea, Korean residents in Japan lost their Japanese citizenship. Failure to define the legal status of the Korean residents has led to many complicated problems. In the light of the unfortunate prewar history between the two nations, Japan should treat the question of Korean residents with sympathy and understanding.

There is hardly any question as to their right of residence in Japan, and understanding has already been reached on their right of permanent residence. The scope of right of permanent residence includes not only those Koreans residing in Japan before the war, but also their offsprings born before the two nations entered into normal diplomatic relations.

On the issue of confirming the nationality of Koreans, in case the Japan-Korea agreement comes into operation, the question still remains whether the validity of the treaty will apply to all Koreans residing in Japan. The Republic of Korea government maintains that since it is the only lawful government in the whole of the Korean Peninsula, the treaty should apply to all the Korean residents in Japan. The Japanese government is opposed to selling out the claims of the Republic of Korea government in the text of the treaty, maintaining that the administrative power of the South Korean government extends only to the area south of 38 degrees North Latitude. Moreover, Japan desires to establish relations with the Republic of Korea as a member of the free world, and believes that it is actually impossible to apply Republic of Korea citizenship to Koreans owing allegiance to North Korea.

Since this question affecting fishing rights and property claim rights is a basic issue in the Japan-Korea negotiations, it is likely to be referred to top level political talks between the two nations.

As part of the property claim, there is the issue of restoring cultural assets. Japan does not believe that she is obligated to make such restitutions, but is willing to a certain degree—in the interest of strengthening friendly relations between the two countries and as a part of cultural cooperation—to meet the wishes of the Korean government.

One important issue which has not been raised at the current negotiations is that of Takeshima Island, claimed by both Japan and Korea but at present occupied by the latter. Assuming that direct talks between the two nations were impossible, the Japanese government in 1954 proposed to refer the matter to the International Court of Justice, but the Korean government refused to entertain the idea. Since it is necessary to obtain Korea's approval before the International Court of Justice will take up the question, there has been no further development on the issue of Takeshima. However, it is the view of the Japanese government that it is necessary to find some concrete basis for the settlement of the issue when diplomatic relations are normalized.

On March 24, 1964, Korean students again demonstrated in the capital city of Seoul against the Japan-Korea talks, sparking off a nationwide movement. Army troops were called out to quell the demonstrations. Having brought down the regime of Syngman Rhee four years earlier, the student demonstrations of South Korea—unlike those of Japan—have the wide support of the citizenry and, consequently, must not be regarded lightly.

The concrete demands of the student demonstrators include the immediate suspension of the Japan-Korea talks and the immediate recall of Chairman Kim. Their opposition to the Japan-Korea talks is at the same time directed against the leader of the Democratic Republic Party, Kim Chong Pil. The people's discontent over the worsening economic conditions in Korea has also added to the fuel.

It is noteworthy that one of the reasons for demanding a halt to the Japan-Korea talks is the charge that the Korean government is negotiating with a humiliating and subservient attitude. The charge of "humiliating" appears to stem from the fact that the property claims right had taken the form of economic cooperation from Japan, whereas, the malcontents assert, Korea has every right to demand such right.

Nevertheless, it is apparent that the demands of the students are also based on highly emotional grounds, such as the absolute defense of the Rhee Line in utter disregard of international law.

Be that as it may, the Civil Rule Party and other opposition parties have organized the "National Struggle Committee Against Humiliating Diplomacy Towards Japan" as part of their movement against the Japan-Korea talks. They vigorously warn that if the present "low posture diplomacy" and the Park-Kim "diplomacy of self-complacency" continue in the future, South Korea's economy, culture and, politics will be in danger of strong Japanese influences.

Mounting student demonstrations finally compelled Kim Chong Pil, who had come to Japan to lend indirect aid to the negotiations, to return to Korea. It is evident that the Korean government had given in to one of the demands of the demonstrators. However, the sudden departure of one of the key figures in Korean politics is not altogether easily understood. It is certainly of great importance that Japan seriously study the background to the latest events in Korea.

While the Park administration has not changed its policy regarding the need to reach a settlement between Japan and Korea, it no doubt feels that, in view of the grave domestic situation, a cooling-off period is essential.

These talks, left in a state of virtual suspension throughout the summer of 1964, were not resumed until December, 1964. In the seventh round of negotiations, the respective committees again went through the routine of discussing the question of the basic relations between Japan and Korea, the question of fisheries and the question of the legal status of Koreans residing in Japan. The discussion did no more than to confirm that the claims and opinions of Japan and Korea remained as sharply divided as ever.

It was under these circumstances that Foreign Minister Shiina Etsusaburo left Tokyo on February 17, 1965, on a four day visit to Seoul, Korea. The Japanese Foreign Minister was cordially greeted by Korean President Park Chung Hee and other high government officials.

Following a series of meetings, the two nations on February 20 agreed on a draft treaty, setting out the basic relations between Japan and Korea. Furthermore, the two nations not only welcomed the action on the treaty as marking a step forward in the normalization of Japan-Korea relations, but also as an impetus to the negotiations on fisheries and other issues which were shortly resumed in Tokyo.

chapter 26

Question of Recognizing Communist China

T HE PROBLEM of Communist China poses the most crucial test for Japan's foreign policy which is unswervingly based on the support of the free world. On January 27, 1964, President Charles de Gaulle created a sensation in international political and diplomatic circles, by extending France's recognition to Communist China.

With this sudden French move, the question of recognizing Communist China began to loom large on Japan's political horizon. The intensity of the debate over Communist China's admission into the United Nations also rose to new heights. The decisive factor in this situation is the question of whether Communist China is a peace loving state. At the present time, there are no perceptible signs that Communist China, which harbors ambitions of world communization, has thrown off her cloak of militancy.

During the Korean War, Communist China intervened militarily on a grand scale. She has repeatedly employed her armed forces in her dispute with India and in the Taiwan Straits. Even today, she is continuing her armed assistance to the guerrillas in South Vietnam and fomenting disorder in Laos.

Moreover, Communist China has not abandoned her policy of liberating Taiwan by force of arms and inflaming the peoples of underdeveloped countries to wage wars of national liberation. Even in their ideological quarrel with the Soviet Union, the Chinese Communist leaders have rejected the Soviet policy of peaceful coexistence, opposed the partial test ban treaty, and chose the path of increasing the membership of the world's nuclear powers.

At this juncture, the fear is remote that Communist China will resort to direct armed aggression against Japan. That Japan is able to feel secure against external threats is attributable to the existence of the Japan-United States Mutual Security Treaty. For her part, Communist China not only vehemently opposes the United States at every turn, but takes every opportunity to emphasize that "U.S. imperialism" is the common enemy of Japan and China.

Chairman Mao Tse-tung has recently attempted to praise anti-American demonstrations staged by a section of Japanese leftists as the patriotic movement of the entire Japanese people, while Premier Chou En-lai has denounced the United States government for mustering its entire strength to prevent the normalization of Japanese-Chinese relations. The object of these Communist Chinese declarations is to alienate Japan and the United States, endeavoring at the same time to destroy the Japan-United States security system. In the face of these onslaughts, Japan must maintain her vigilance.

In April, 1952, Japan concluded the Sino-Japanese Peace Treaty with the Nationalist government of Taiwan, establishing diplomatic relations and recognizing it as the de jure government of China. By entering into this peace treaty, the state of war between Japan and China was concluded and Japan reaffirmed that she had relinquished claims to

Taiwan and the Pescadores as stipulated in the San Francisco Treaty of Peace.

President Chiang Kai-shek, for his part, renounced all rights to claim any compensation from Japan. Japan is deeply indebted to Generalissimo Chiang Kai-shek who, on the occasion of the termination of the war, issued a proclamation to "repay enmity with virtue," and safely repatriated more than two million Japanese soldiers from the Chinese mainland.

Needless to say, Japan, in concluding the treaty of peace with the Nationalist government of China, recognized it as the de jure government of China with which she had been at war. The treaty, therefore, terminated the state of war between Japan and China and settled the question of reparations—a question which Japan has no intention of reopening with the government of Communist China.

France, which recognized the Chinese Communist regime, has been strangely silent about the true nature of her relations with the Nationalist Chinese government. At a subsequent press conference, President de Gaulle, while paying his respects to President Chiang Kai-shek for his patriotic spirit, went no further than to praise the Chinese People's Republic as a great nation. He refused to elaborate.

Undoubtedly, the French President was deliberately non-committal. One reason may be that, although Japan did renounce her rights to Taiwan under the San Francisco Treaty, the country of its reversion remained indefinite. Thus, the legal status of Taiwan is a sensitive issue. France reportedly recognized Communist China on the principle of "One China," a principle which at the same time did not absolutely rule out the contention of "One China and Taiwan." She preferred to let time solve the question of her relations with the Nationalist Chinese.

On February 10, just two weeks after the French diplomatic move, the Nationalist Chinese government in a retaliatory
action, severed its ties with France. The Nationalist Chinese
felt that if they continued to retain relations with France,
it would be tantamount to recognizing the existence of
"One China and One Taiwan," an original view held by
France. This view could also be interpreted as accepting
the two-China theory, a theory which Nationalist China
could not possibly accept. Accordingly, Nationalist China,
in carrying out its diplomatic break with France, took a
predetermined policy which simultaneously forestalled the
French from making the first move.

Meanwhile, opinion was growing in Japan that efforts
should be made to urge Nationalist China not to sever ties
with France, fearing that such a drastic step would lower
the international prestige of Nationalist China and en-
danger its seat in the United Nations. Influential personalities in the United States also held similar views. To President Chiang Kai-shek, a man of principles, this situation
was naturally unbearable. In this crisis for Taipei, the
United States government adopted a sympathetic attitude.
President Chiang's move, however, was a heavy blow
against advocates of the principle of "One China, One
Taiwan."

For Communist China, the question of admission to the
United Nations is essentially a matter of Communist China
replacing Nationalist China. This so-called issue of representation of China in the United Nations is a long outstanding controversy.

Shortly after the Chinese Communist government was
established on October 1, 1949, Foreign Minister Chou
En-lai dispatched a telegram to the President of the Fourth
United Nations General Assembly, repudiating the legal
status of the representative of Nationalist China, who.

according to Chou, no longer spoke on behalf of the people of China. In the period up to September 18, 1950, following this notification, Foreign Minister Chou En-lai sent several more telegrams and letters to the members of the Security Council, the United Nations General Assembly president, and the Secretary General of the United Nations, demanding that the Nationalist Chinese delegate be expelled and be replaced by a representative of Communist China at the sessions of the General Assembly.

This question of Chinese representation appeared on the agenda of the United Nations for the first time at the Fifth General Assembly meeting in 1950. Although India and the Soviet Union separately presented resolutions demanding that Communist China replace Nationalist China as representative of China, they failed to get the necessary support.

During the decade between 1951 to 1960, the issue of Chinese Communist representation remained in abeyance as a result of the acceptance of the United States recommendation that "the General Assembly should not decide to exclude representatives of Nationalist China from the Assembly or to seat representatives of Communist China to represent China in the Assembly."

As the number of nations opposing or abstaining from this recommendation gradually grew, the United States proposed at the 16th General Assembly session in 1961 that the question of the representation of China be raised as an important question within the context of Article 18 of the Charter of the United Nations. The United States proposal was, in effect, an attempt to regard any change in the representation of China as an important question, in which case a two-third majority would be required in accordance with Article 18 of the Charter.

A five-power resolution, embodying this principle, was

presented by the United States, Australia, Italy, Colombia, and Japan, and formally adopted by the world body. At the same time, the General Assembly rejected a draft resolution submitted by the Soviet Union to oust the delegate of Nationalist China from the United Nations and allow the delegate of the People's Republic of China to be seated as the lawful representative. At the following General Assembly session of the United Nations in 1962, an identical resolution introduced by the Soviet Union was defeated. A similar fate met the joint resolution of Albania and Cambodia in 1963 to unseat the Chinese Nationalist representative.

It was earlier anticipated that France's recognition of Communist China would considerably increase the number of votes at the United Nations in favor of the Peking regime. However, the majority of the twelve states of the Brazzaville Group has shown no indication of following France's lead. In fact, both Malagasy (Madagascar) and Cameroon have stated categorically that they would not recognize Communist China.

The number of countries recognizing Communist China as of March, 1964, stood at 48, while those having diplomatic ties with Nationalist China totaled 62, with nine countries having no relations with either of the two governments.

Under the circumstances, should any resolution be presented to unseat the Nationalist Chinese representative in favor of Communist China at the 1964–65 session of the United Nations, the possibility of its passage still remains dubious, although voting in support of the former may dwindle to a certain extent. Even if the resolution were adopted, it is not unlikely that the United States will assert the continuing validity of the resolution of the 16th General

Assembly, that the question of the representation of China be regarded as an important question.

If, for argument's sake, the United States position were questioned by other members of the United Nations, it would still require a two-thirds majority to vote down this American stand on the validity of the 1961 decision. Thus, it is quite apparent that, in view of the number of road-blocks, the issue of Chinese representation will not be settled by a single act.

Furthermore, if the principle of "important question" should be overruled, in the future there would still remain the important question of Chinese representation in the Security Council. Whether this question of recognition of representation warrants the use of the veto as a permanent member of the Security Council, or whether the issue can be resolved by a simple majority vote, remains in doubt. If the right of veto is recognized, theoretically it could result in a strange situation in which China's seat in the Security Council is occupied by a representative of Nationalist China, while the seat in the General Assembly is held by the delegate of Communist China.

Ever since France recognized the Communist Chinese government, Prime Minister Ikeda and Foreign Minister Ohira have reiterated that Japan will seek a fair solution of the question of China within the framework of the United Nations and will abide by the mainstream of world public opinion. Later, in his reply to a question in the House of Representatives, Foreign Minister Ohira declared that "should a situation arise in which Communist China becomes a legitimate member of the United Nations with the blessing of its members, Japan will have to consider normalizing diplomatic relations with Communist China." This statement became a subject of dispute, but it was made on the premise that Communist China was unanimously welcomed into the world forum as a peace loving state.

It is neither possible nor feasible for Japan to ignore the existence of Communist China which has held sway over the mainland for over 14 years and maintains jurisdictional control over some 600 million people. The Japanese government has, on the basis of separating politics and economics, exerted efforts in the direction of expanding trade and exchange of personnel between the two countries. For Japan, the question of China remains a matter of paramount importance, a matter which must be handled with the utmost care and discretion. The government is fully aware that any hasty conclusion may have disastrous consequences.

In view of the gravity of the situation, I focused my questions on China during the interpellations on Japan's foreign policy on March 1, 1964, in the Budget Committee of the House of Councillors. A summary of the exchange which I had with Prime Minister Ikeda and Foreign Minister Ohira on the occasion, will no doubt serve to throw some light on the official views held by the government, as well as my own views on how the vital problem of China should be handled.

In opening my interpellations, I inquired as to the imminence of Communist China's admission into the United Nations and the related effects of France's recognition of Communist China. In reply, Foreign Minister Ohira revealed that, except for Congo Brazzaville which had followed France's example, other countries of the world were relatively unperturbed. He could not, therefore, anticipate what form the question of Chinese representation would take in the forthcoming United Nations General Assembly.

In his reply, Prime Minister Ikeda pointed to the fact that at the general meeting of the World Health Organization on March 3, 1964, when the issue of Communist

China's admission was debated, the number of votes in support of Peking had actually dwindled, compared to the voting of the previous year. In the WHO tally, 51 countries had supported Nationalist China, 21 had opposed, and 22 had abstained. The number of nations favoring Peking's entry had actually fallen by one half over the preceding year and the number of countries abstaining had nearly doubled.

Analyzing the United States government's policy toward Asia, I expressed the view that all pertinent information indicated that this policy would not be altered. In this connection, I quoted James Reston, New York Times correspondent in Washington, who had asseverated that there is no need to re-examine the policy of containment toward the communist countries, and that the policy itself is not out of date.

Affirming my analysis, Foreign Minister Ohira declared: "The American government's policy toward China has not undergone any fundamental change at all. I think we should correctly evaluate America's strength, role, and achievements in contributing to the stability and prosperity of East Asia."

Amplifying my views further, I asserted that "if there is no substantial change in the attitude of the United States government, I do not think it is necessary for Japan to change its existing attitude. But, on the other hand, I think it is unnatural and imprudent to permanently refuse recognition of Communist China, or to remain adamantly opposed to the normalization of our relationship. As our relations have been inseparably linked politically, economically, and culturally from time immemorial, Japan should, considering its own position and if certain preconditions are met, move towards recognition and normalization of relations."

I then referred to basic preconditions for the recognition of Communist China. I urged that as the first step, Communist China should recognize the Japan-United States Mutual Security Treaty; secondly, should respect the Japan-China Peace Treaty; thirdly, should renounce the right to claim reparations from Japan; and, fourthly, under the principles of non-intervention in other's internal affairs, should promise not to engage in communist subversive propaganda or undertake indirect aggression against Japan.

Replying to my query, Prime Minister Ikeda said: "My opinions are identical to those of Mr. Kajima. I am not averse to considering the matter at a time when Communist China demonstrates that she is not warlike and truly takes the initiative in cooperating for the peace of Asia and the peace of the world, a fact which is accepted not only by China, but other nations as well."

The acceptance by Prime Minister Ikeda and other leading personalities of the four preconditions for the recognition of Communist China, has been for me a source of deep satisfaction and encouragement.

Furthermore, I voiced the desire of Japan to become a permanent member of the Security Council, pointing out that: "In the event Communist China is welcomed as a member of the United Nations, it is generally anticipated that she will become not just a member, but at the same time a permanent member of the United Nations Security Council. In such a case, if Japan remains merely a member and is unable to acquire permanent membership in the Security Council, its position will be inferior to Communist China, politically, economically, and socially. From the standpoint of maintaining our national pride and our national interest, I do not think that this can be tolerated. I feel that Japan should achieve permanent membership in the Security Council either before Communist China sits in the Security Council as a permanent member, or, at least at the same time."

In connection with this question, I raised the issue concerning the need to amend the present Charter of the United Nations.

Responding to the latter question, Foreign Minister Ohira said: "I quite agree with you. Unfortunately, however, owing to the entanglements involved in the issue of Chinese representation, the Soviet Union at the present time shows no inclination of being ready to act in concert with us. Despite the complicated situation, I feel that it is unquestionably our responsibility to make the necessary efforts hand in hand with the ripening of world public opinion in that direction."

I referred next to the question of the articles relating to former enemy states contained in the United Nations Charter, and stated that Japan should propose the invalidation of those articles.

I mentioned that the related Articles 53 and 107 of the Charter included an important exception to the principle that "no enforcement action shall be taken under regional arrangements or by regional agencies without the authorization of the Security Council." In the light of these two exceptions, especially the latter, the Sino-Soviet Treaty of Alliance, Friendship and Mutual Assistance of February 14, 1950, is legal.

Replying to my question, Foreign Minister Ohira said: "We believe that it would be most appropriate to place this question on the agenda—for study within the framework of the Charter as a whole—of the preparatory committee for the plenary meeting which is to study the time and method of reexamining the United Nations Charter on the occasion of the 20th General Assembly." He added that: "Although it is possible for the Charter to be amended by ordinary procedures of amendment, we regret that at the present time realization is very difficult, so long as the Soviet Union is maintaining its attitude of opposition to the plenary meeting for the reexamination of the United Nations Charter."

Among the four preconditions for the recognition of Communist China, I believe the question of renouncing the right to claim reparations from Japan is more complex than it appears on the surface. As stated earlier, while the Japanese government assumes that this question is already settled, Communist China does not recognize Nationalist China's right to speak on its behalf on reparations from Japan or, for that matter, even the validity of the Japan-China Peace Treaty. However, Premier Chou En-lai declared in July, 1955, that "Communist China reserves the right to claim reparations from Japan to compensate the Chinese people who are unable to forget the incalculable losses and sufferings at the hands of the Japanese militarists." Chou did not mention any specific sum, but it is believed to amount to tens of billions of dollars. One leading official of Communist China is reported to have disclosed that the sum under consideration amounts to an astronomical figure of five thousand billion dollars.

Needless to say, payment of such a stupendous sum for reparations would impose an intolerable burden on the Japanese economy. At the same time, it can be expected that Communist China, by reserving the right to claim reparations from Japan, could wield this threat as a powerful trump card in any serious negotiations she might in the future conduct with Japan. In other words, Communist China might conceivably—in exchange for Japan's neutalization and severance of her military links with the United States—show willingness to drastically reduce her reparation demands.

In any event, Japan should be adequately prepared to meet major obstacles in any effort to promote diplomatic ties with Communist China, the thorny question of reparations being only one of them.

chapter 27

Relations with Chinese Nationalist Government

THE POSITION of Taiwan (Formosa) is a very important key to the peace of Asia. To understand the true nature of the relations between Japan and Nationalist China, it is necessary to review some of the outstanding developments prior to the conclusion of the Sino-Japanese Peace Treaty.

The Chinese Nationalist government, under the leadership of Generalissimo Chiang Kai-shek, fled in December, 1949, from the Chinese mainland to the island of Taiwan. In view of the existence of two rival governments claiming to be the true representatives of the whole of China, the Chinese delegate was excluded from the San Francisco Peace Conference. Japan was, therefore, left with the freedom to choose either Nationalist China or Communist China to be the other party in concluding peace with Japan.

According to the recollections of Yoshida Shigeru, then Prime Minister, Japan adopted the cautious policy of welcoming friendly and intimate economic relations with Taiwan, but at the same time, avoiding any form of ties with Taiwan which would probably meet with the strong disapproval of the newly established communist regime in Peking. However, Japan had to acknowledge the fact that it was the Nationalist government with which she had been in a state of hostilities from the outset, and the latter's position in the United Nations was of immense significance. With the subsequent large-scale intervention of Communist China in the Korean War, Japan had no longer an alternative in selecting a party to the peace treaty relating to China.

Another unexpected development was the stand taken by the United States Senate, making Japan's choice of a Chinese regime a precondition for ratifying the San Francisco peace treaty. Faced with a new dilemma, the Japanese government felt that it could no longer delay, at the expense of non-ratification of the San Francisco peace treaty, its decision on which of the two Chinese governments to recognize.

On his fourth and timely visit to Japan in December, 1951, John Foster Dulles, special envoy of President Harry S. Truman, had as his main mission the acceleration of Japan's decision to choose Nationalist China as the representative government of China. Apparently his mission was successful as Prime Minister Yoshida in his letter to Dulles affirmed that "Japan has no intention of concluding a bilateral treaty with Communist China," and assured him that "Japan is ready to normalize relations with the Nationalist government in accordance with the principles laid down in the San Francisco peace treaty."

At the same time, Prime Minister Yoshida clarified Japan's policy of limited peace by stating in his letter that "the stipulations of the treaty to be signed between Japan and the Nationalist government will apply to all territories now governed and that would be governed in future by Nationalist China."

On the basis of this decision, in February, 1952, the

Yoshida Cabinet sent Kawada Retsu, Japan's plenipotentiary, to Taipei to open negotiations with Yeh Kung-chao, China's plenipotentiary. Consequently, after prolonged parleys of nearly three months the Sino-Japanese Peace Treaty was finally concluded on April 28, the same day as the effectuation of the San Francisco peace treaty. The statement that the Nationalist government had voluntarily renounced its right to claim reparations from Japan was included in the attached protocol, and Japan's reference to the limited peace with the Nationalist government was dovetailed into the Treaty through the exchange of notes.

In any event, it is an irrefutable fact that the conclusion of this peace treaty with the Nationalist government, despite its character of limited peace, legally terminated the state of war with the whole of China and established peaceful relations between the two nations.

In accordance with the stipulations of the San Francisco peace treaty, Japan renounced all her rights, title and claim to Taiwan and the Pescadores in the Sino-Japanese Peace Treaty. The ultimate country of reversion, however, of these areas was not regulated in either the San Francisco peace treaty or the Sino-Japanese Peace Treaty. This fact has given rise to the general view among the former Allied Powers that the formal reversion of Taiwan has yet to be determined.

The circumstances under which Taiwan and the Pescadores were transferred to the Nationalist government are involved. During World War II, in November, 1943, when the leaders of the United States, Great Britain and China met at Cairo to discuss the solution of the problem of Japan, it was agreed that Taiwan and the Pescadores should be restored to China. This agreement was confirmed in the Potsdam Agreement drafted by these three powers and later signed by the Soviet Union in July, 1945.

Both the Cairo and Potsdam declarations did not legally regulate the transfer of the territorial rights over Taiwan. They merely contained general principles governing the disposition of Japanese territories preparatory to the conclusion of the peace treaty with Japan. General MacArthur, in his capacity of Supreme Commander of Allied Powers, conferred on the representative of Generalissimo Chiang Kai-shek the right of accepting the surrender of the Japanese armed forces on Taiwan. This mission enabled the Nationalist government to assume physical control over Taiwan and the neighboring islands.

It is universally acknowledged that postwar territorial disposition comes in to effect legally for the first time only when stipulations of the peace treaty are confirmed by international law. By this definition, the legal status of Taiwan has not yet been fully established. Only the former Allied Powers who accepted Japan's surrender are vested with the right of determining its possession, but as of now, the Allied Powers, including the Soviet Union, have failed to reach any decision on the final disposition of the territories in question.

Notwithstanding these circumstances, the Nationalist government and Communist China, while completely at loggerheads over all other issues, are firmly united in their stand that Taiwan is an inseparable territory of China.

Taiwan and the Pescadores, according to the claim of the Nationalist government, were originally a part of China, ceded by China to Japan under the provisions of the Treaty of Shimonoseki of 1895, which marked the end of the Sino-Japanese War. In December, 1941, by formally proclaiming war against Japan, China served notice that she was renouncing all treaties between Japan and China. By asserting that Japanese rule over Taiwan has lost its validity, Nationalist China assured herself of the right to exercise her proclamation into action when Japan capitulated to the Allied Powers.

Nationalist China also insists that the restoration of Taiwan and the other islands of China had already been confirmed in the Cairo and Potsdam Declarations. Communist China, on the other hand, has been loudly clamoring that the liberation of Taiwan, an integral part of China, is an internal question, allowing no interference on the part of the United Nations or any other country. Insofar as Japan is concerned, having irrevocably renounced her territorial right to Taiwan, she is now in a position of a third power, devoid of any right to speak on the matter.

Undeniably, in the last resort, the fate of Nationalist China has been inseparably bound with that of the United States ever since its transfer to Taiwan from the Chinese mainland. No sooner had Generalissimo Chiang Kai-shek transferred his capital to Taipei, then President Truman in January, 1950, announced that the United States would extend economic assistance to Taiwan, but would remain free from any military involvement.

With the outbreak of the Korean War, however, President Truman issued a statement declaring the neutralization of Taiwan and its defense by the United States Seventh Fleet. At the same time, the United States appealed to Nationalist China to suspend any attack against the mainland. The problem of defending Taiwan became even more acute when Red China openly intervened in the Korean War. In the light of these developments, the United States and Nationalist China concluded a military assistance agreement in February, 1951, followed by a dispatch of a United States military advisory group to Taiwan.

When General Dwight Eisenhower assumed the presidency of the United States, the operational duties of the United States Seventh Fleet were modified in February,

1953, and the declaration of the neutralization of Taiwan was rescinded. Somewhat later, in December, 1954, the Nationalist government signed a mutual defense treaty with the United States, in which the latter clearly pledged to assist Taiwan in the event of any attack by an aggressor against Taiwan and the Pescadores.

To enable the United States to fulfill its defense obligations, the Nationalist government bestowed upon the United States the right to establish army, navy, and air force bases within Taiwan and its adjacent islands. This treaty, in effect, gave the United States backing to Nationalist Chinese control over the territory of Taiwan. Thus, a new significant treaty affecting the West Pacific area came into being. Since then, the United States has expended the huge sum of three billion dollars in both military and economic assistance to Nationalist China.

Just prior to the conclusion of this defense treaty, minor skirmishes had taken place in March, 1954, between the frontline troops stationed in Quemoy and other offshore islands (Nationalist China's outposts near Fukien Province) and the Chinese Communist forces. The situation became even more ominous when the Communist forces suddenly opened up a heavy harrage on Quemoy in September and subsequently forced the Nationalist troops to evacuate from Ichiangshan Island in January, and Tachen Island in February, 1955. To meet the increasingly heavy Communist pressures, Nationalist China has been making every possible effort to defend its bastions of Quemoy and Matsu.

These two islands are situated only three to six miles off the Chinese mainland, and Quemoy faces Amoy, one of China's major ports. The United States, which once urged the Nationalist government to evacuate from Tachen Island, has not suggested any similar retreat from Quemoy and Matsu. In addition, the United States congress later passed a resolution declaring that the United States would take every measure to defend these islands, in case the President recognized the attack against Quemoy and Matsu as part of a general attack against Taiwan and the Pescadores.

Nonetheless, the United States has continued to discourage any attempts by the Nationalist government to launch a counter-offensive against the Chinese mainland. When tension in the Taiwan Straits reached new heights, in the wake of the resumption of heavy Communist artillery bombardment of Quemoy in August, 1958, U.S. Secretary of State Dulles hurriedly paid a visit to Taiwan in October. Following a series of urgent meetings between Dulles and Chiang Kai-shek, a joint statement was issued declaring that the restoration of liberty on the Chinese mainland should be attained, not through force of arms, but by the application of the Three People's Principles.

Digressing a little, let us turn to the subject of the Three People's Principles. The guiding principles of the Nationalist Party, first advocated by the father of the Chinese Revolution, Sun Wen or Sun Yat-sen, constitute the three principles of the people, the people's right, and the people's livelihood. The Republic of China, however, enforced a new constitution under Generalissimo Chiang Kai-shek in 1947, upholding the three principles—the people's right, social peace, and the people's welfare—as the fundamentals of the republican form of government. The Three People's Principles, as advocated by the Generalissimo, refer to the latter principles.

The Nationalist government has been taking every opportunity to express its strong determination to fight to the last in the defense of both Quemoy and Matsu, primarily for political and psychological reasons, rather than military. Although the possession of the Quemoy and Matsu islands is not indispensable to the defense of Taiwan, their occupation by the Nationalist Chinese forces is a symbol of their resolve to carry out the promise of returning to the mainland.

Strangely enough, among the leaders of Communist China there is said to exist an opinion that the temporary occupation of these islands by the Nationalist army is also advantageous to Communist China. Professor Scalapino of the University of California also holds a similar view. According to Professor Scalapino, while it is understandable that Communist China would not welcome heavy losses in manpower from a frontal assault on these islands, the acquisition of the islands by Communist China would increase the forcefulness of the theory of "One China, one Taiwan." It might, at the same time, conceivably impair the will of the Chinese Nationalists to continue the civil war.

In his television debate with the Republican candidate Richard Nixon during the 1960 presidential campaign, John F. Kennedy proposed a retreat from Quemoy and Matsu by Nationalist China. After taking over his post as American President in 1961, Kennedy did not modify the policy hitherto pursued by the United States. Lyndon Johnson, then Vice-President, who visited Taiwan in May of the same year, even issued a joint statement with President Chiang Kai-shek in which the United States declared that she had no intention of recognizing the Communist regime in Peking, opposed Communist China's entry into the United Nations, and reaffirmed the importance of the position of Nationalist China in the United Nations. Needless to say, this United States attitude was in no way affected by France's recognition of Communist China in January, 1964.

Before shifting the seat of his government to Taiwan, Generalissimo Chiang Kai-shek had earlier announced his retirement in January, 1949, in order to facilitate peace negotiations with the Chinese communists. Called upon to lead the struggle against the onrushing communist tide in China, Generalissimo Chiang Kai-shek returned to active duty in March, 1950, and was subsequently reelected President in April, 1954. In February, 1960, he accepted the presidential office for the third term. Taiwan, now virtually under the one party rule of the Kuomintang, displays the slogan "recover the mainland" in every town and village throughout the island.

Notwithstanding the emergency situation, Taiwan has made outstanding progress in all fields of activities, especially in economic development. The island has recovered from the serious drop in production which followed the postwar repatriation of Japanese specialists and attending industrial dislocations. The level of production has steadily risen with the growing power of the Nationalist government.

In sharp contrast to the disastrous failures of the "great leap forward" program of the communist administration on the mainland, Taiwan has registered an economic expansion which is the envy of other developing nations. The land reform program on Taiwan, hailed as a notable success, brought nearly 90 per cent of the entire cultivated area under the control of the tillers of the soil.

Statistically, the results of economic construction in Taiwan reveal that agricultural production has increased by three and a half times, and industrial production by thirteen times as against the increase in population of 89 per cent in 1962 compared with 1946. During the period from 1950 to 1960, the people's real income had doubled and the volume of electricity consumption, a yardstick for measuring national prosperity, had increased fourfold.

Under the present circumstances, Generalissimo Chiang Kai-shek has no alternative but to stress the overriding importance of political power, with less emphasis on military power, as a means of launching a counteroffensive. In other words, Chiang Kai-shek is fashioning Taiwan into a model province based on the Three People's Principles, economically and politically, hoping that this growing political power will foster the people's resistance against the communist regime.

The Nationalist government is keenly aware, however, that they cannot launch a successful attack against the communists who rule the people of the mainland with a mailed fist without resorting to military force. It is understandable, therefore, that the Generalissimo advocated a political and military counter-offensive against Communist China at a seven-three ratio.

In order to realize its national salvation, however, Taiwan faces tremendous hardships and difficulties. In the first place, she must bear the heavy pressure of military expenditures, accounting for more than half of the total budget. The Nationalist government is only able to shoulder its financial burdens by relying on substantial United States assistance of nearly one-third of its annual budget. During the past ten years, United States military assistance has averaged nearly $200,000,000 a year and economic assistance about $100,000,000. Meanwhile, the United States has threatened to reduce its economic assistance, on the ground that Taiwan has become economically self-supporting and it has become imperative for the United States to stop the heavy flow of dollars abroad.

It would be unwise to ignore the question of nationality in any discussion concerning Taiwan. Of the total population of 12,000,000 on Taiwan, over 9,000,000 people who had settled on the provincial island from the 13th Century to the 19th Century are now being discriminately treated from the approximately 2,000,000 mainland Chinese who had sought refuge in Taiwan together with the Nationalist government. Violently reacting against the discrimination practiced by the new arrivals, the native people of Taiwan staged the so-called 2.28 riot in February, 1947, on a massive scale against the Nationalist government. The riot was thoroughly crushed and the leaders severely punished.

As the island's economic condition took a turn for the better, relations between the natives of the province and the people from the mainland began to improve. Nevertheless, noticeably very few people born on the island of Taiwan have risen to responsible posts in the central government. At present, only two cabinet ministers are native-born, but their posts are relatively unimportant. The native-born also hold only 30 per cent of all government positions, while in the armed forces they have not been promoted above the rank of field grade officers. In ten or twenty years the situation on Taiwan is bound to change radically as people from the mainland fade from the local scene and as the younger generation comes to the fore.

A view prevails in certain circles that the future of Taiwan should be entrusted to the free will of the people of Taiwan. This opinion more or less coincides with the long-range view regarding the ultimate destiny of Taiwan. It also fits in with the theory of "One China, One Taiwan." William J. Fullbright, Chairman of the U.S. Senate Foreign Relations Committee, emphasized his theory of "One China, One Taiwan" in a speech to congress March 25, 1964. In his speech and in his statements at a press conference which followed, he said that Taiwan should be given its independence. His remarks attracted widespread interest.

With the death of Vice President Chen Cheng on March 5, 1965, the probability of Chiang Ching-kuo, a Cabinet Minister and son of Chiang Kai-shek, succeeding the aging President appears increasingly likely. However, the power struggle that has been taking place for years will not come out into the open so long as the Generalissimo remains in good health.

In June, 1957, Prime Minister Kishi visited Taiwan, the first Japanese Premier to pay an official visit, and held a lengthy talk with the Generalissimo, initiating closer ties between Japan and the Nationalist government. On this occasion, the Japan-China Cooperative Committee was duly established with the participation of influential members from political and financial circles of both countries. In the field of trade between Japan and China, the first formal trade agreement was signed in September, 1950, prior to the conclusion of the peace treaty, which has since been renewed every year on a planned basis.

Meanwhile, as trade relations between Japan and Communist China developed, Japan could not avoid inviting the displeasure of the Nationalist government. The issue of the expanding trade relations between Japan and Communist China rapidly assumed serious proportions when in the fall of 1962 the so-called L.T. Formula (abbreviations for the names of Takasaki Tatsunosuke, Japanese representative, and Liao Cheng-chih, Communist China's representative) for the boosting of the two-way trade was adopted. This formula extended trading opportunities to firms other than those regarded hitherto as "friendly." The Nationalist government suspended negotiations for a loan of $10,000,000 from Japan in protest.

Following up the official protest, the Nationalist government recalled its Ambassador to Japan, Chang Li-sheng, as soon as Japan approved the export of a vinylon plant on the basis of an extended payment to Communist China. Although the above measures were taken by the Japanese government after careful consideration, Nationalist China assumed a stubborn attitude toward Japan, asserting that "the Japanese approval to export a vinylon plant to Communist China was tantamount to Japanese assistance to Communist China, just at a time when the industrial development of Communist China was being retarded by the abrupt termination of Soviet technical assistance, stemming from the Sino-Soviet ideological dispute." Moreover, Nationalist China felt that the Japanese government should pay special regard to the claim and position of Nationalist China in view of their special relationship. The Nationalist Chinese also found it difficult to believe that Japan could be so absorbed in her own economic development as to forget the danger which communism posed for Japan's security.

Then in September, the report of an interview given to an executive of the Hearst Newspapers of America by Prime Minister Ikeda, in which the latter was erroneously quoted as having stated that the counteroffensive of the Nationalist government would be hopeless, bitterly incensed the authorities in Taipei.

Adding fuel to the fire was the case of Chou Hung-ching, an interpreter for the Communist Chinese Oil Pressure Apparatus Mission to Japan, who sought refuge in the Soviet embassy in Tokyo in October. After being handed over to the Japanese authorities, Chou Hung-ching first voiced his desire to go to Taiwan, then, just as suddenly, revealed his desire to stay in Japan. While the authorities were attempting to clarify his intentions, Chou expressed his wish to return to his homeland. Notwithstanding the fact that the Japanese government was handling the case on the basis of respecting the free will of Chou Hung-ching who finally decided to return to Communist China, the Nationalist government strongly felt that it would be inhuman to send back a refugee to Communist China, and blatantly accused the Japanese government of cooperating with the brainwashing maneuvers of Communist China, an act which Taipei charged finally induced Chou Hung-ching to return to the Communist-held mainland.

To allay the offended feelings of the government in Taiwan, Japan deliberately held up the repatriation of Chou Hung-ching to Communist China, and, as a further measure to explain her position, dispatched Mr. Ohno Bamboku, vice-president of the Liberal Democratic Party, to Taiwan as a special envoy of Prime Minister Ikeda on the occasion of the 76th birthday of Generalissimo Chiang Kai-shek on October 31, 1963.   The Nationalist Government, however, remained unconvinced, and recalled Chang Po-chien, Charge d'Affaires of the Chinese embassy, and other senior embassy officials to Taiwan early in January, 1964, as soon as the departure permit for Chou Hung-ching was issued by the Japanese government. The Taiwan government also suspended all purchases of Japanese goods.

French recognition of Communist China somewhat eased the anti-Japanese feelings of Nationalist China, but the government did not readily change its stiff attitude. It is quite natural, therefore, that Foreign Minister Ohira urged the importance of relations between Japan and Nationalist China before seriously considering the question pending between Japan and Communist China.

Then, at the end of February, Yoshida Shigeru, former Prime Minister, visited Generalissimo Chiang Kai-shek in Taiwan in his individual capacity. Their cordial exchange of views on the future outlook of Asia as well as the role of both Japan and China in the world of tomorrow, ranging far and wide, is of profound significance.

Immediately after his return to Japan, the Japanese elder statesman stated that the internal situation in Taiwan and the people's livelihood have been stabilized far more than he had imagined. The island had a surplus of over 14 million bushels of rice. Production of the fishery, forestry, sugar, and other industries was continuing to expand. Commenting on the trading relations between Japan and Communist China, a source of irritation to Nationalist China, Yoshida pointed to the fact that Communist China is importing food and raw cotton on the basis of an extended payment, its population was increasing by 12 million a year, with its rulers dedicated to the goals of militant communism. Conducting trade with a nation under these circumstances, he said, could hardly augur well for Japan. Instead, Japan should exert her efforts towards establishing good neighborly relations with Korea and Taiwan, and contribute to the stability and development of these two nations.

When in March, 1964, Mori Matsuhei, Parliamentary Vice-Minister for Foreign Affairs, visited Taiwan and urged resumption of normal relations, the Nationalist government responded by appointing Chen Tse-hua, Consul-General in Yokohama, to the post of Charge d'Affaires of the Chinese embassy in Tokyo.

chapter 28

Japan's
Economic Diplomacy

E CONOMIC issues are no less important than the maintenance of national security in influencing a country's foreign policy today. This is particularly true in the case of Japan which has only a very limited area, insignificant natural resources, and, an overpopulation problem. Having no other means to sustain such a large population except through free and equal trade, Japan rightfully places paramount importance on her economic diplomacy.

Moreover, in a broader sense, the economic issues are included in the maintenance of security. While the fear of an atomic holocaust has engendered a mood of rapprochement between the United States and the Soviet Union against the bitter background of confrontation between the free world and the communist bloc, their struggle in the economic sphere has notably accelerated. The so-called policy of peaceful coexistence initiated by Soviet Premier Khrushchev is nothing more than an all-out economic struggle between the two opposing world camps. As the disavowal of war gained in intensity, the crucial battle between the two inveterate opponents began shifting increasingly to the economic front.

Furthermore, Premier Khrushchev himself has repeatedly stressed the importance of the non-military element in the communist aggression, and has also on a number of occasions reiterated his confidence in the final victory of communism through non-military means. This is a clear warning of the dangers inherent in the economic offensive launched by the communist bloc.

The main stage of East-West confrontation has been developing in the less-developed countries of the world. There are signs, too, that the center of the cold war is also moving into these critical areas.

The postwar Japanese economic diplomacy began with the settlement of the reparations issue. However, the fact should not be overlooked that most of the countries demanding reparations were also countries that were underdeveloped, making the question of assisting the underdeveloped countries closely allied to the payment of reparations.

Japanese economic diplomacy is designed to meet this major trend in the international situation in intimate collaboration with other free countries. This broadly based cooperation is carried out in the field of trade and commerce through various agencies of the United Nations, such as GATT (General Agreements on Tariffs and Trade), IMF (International Monetary Fund) and ECAFE (Economic Commission for Asia and the Far East), and in the field of assistance to underdeveloped countries cooperating with other countries concerned through the United Nations, the Colombo Plan and DAC (Development Assistance Commission), a subsidiary organization of the OECD (Organization for Economic Cooperation and Development.)

The Japanese economy has been steadily expanding in line with the government policy of doubling the income within ten years. Since prospects for future expansion are also reassuring, Japan's position in the international economic community is also continuously rising.

In his speech in the National Diet in January, 1964, Prime Minister Ikeda declared that the government intended to contribute positively towards the development of the world economy in close cooperation with the free countries. In other words, he pledged to strive to strengthen and expand the so-called open economic system.

As a member of GATT, Japan assumed the position of an Article 11 nation in February, 1963, a status which forbids import controls based on international balance of payments. In its relations with IMF, Japan also advanced on April 1, 1964, to an Article 8 country, which prevents a country from imposing currency controls on grounds of international balance of payment difficulties. With these developments, Japan's economy can be said to have attained maturity in the international economic society.

Japan also formally joined the OECD in May, an organization composed of industrially advanced Western nations capable of giving a lead to international economic trends. Immediately on attaining maturity, Japan leaped into the position of a leader. Being the only nation in Asia to have attained the position of an industrially advanced nation, her responsibilities are indeed of vital importance.

The Japanese government in its announcement on assuming the status of Article 8 of the IMF declared: "On this occasion, the government is pushing ahead with preparations to formally seek membership of the OECD, demonstrating that it has arrived at a stage where it is in a position to join the other advanced nations of the world in adopting a positive free economy." It added that "epochal significance of a free and open economy is the closer economic exchange with other foreign countries and the increasingly greater benefits from sharing in international cooperation."

On the other hand, the move towards a free economy signified that Japan's economy is directly influenced by international economic forces. It is, therefore, essential that both government and people, recognizing the importance of Japan's responsibility towards the world economy, should appropriately adapt themselves to the new situation.

Japan also participated in the United Nations Trade and Development Conference which began in Geneva on March 23, 1964. In addition, the Kennedy Round of negotiations aimed at reducing tariffs under GATT is bound to test Japan's overseas economic activities.

As a direct consequence of her disastrous defeat in World War II, Japan has had to overcome tremendous difficulties and handicaps before being readmitted to the international economic society. In order to realize the object of broadly enjoying commercial relations on the basis of equality and reciprocity with other nations, Japan eagerly became a member of GATT and signed treaties of commerce and navigation.

However, there are not a few countries—among them Britain and France—which continue to deny equal treatment to Japan. The removal of such discriminatory barriers still faces Japan's economic diplomacy with a serious challenge.

It was under these circumstances that the Anglo-Japanese Treaty of Commerce and Navigation was concluded in November, 1962, followed in May, 1963, by the Franco-Japanese Commercial Agreement. It is to the great credit of our economic diplomacy that shortly thereafter the

Western European countries, including Britain and France, agreed not to apply article 35 of GATT against Japan.

Article 35 of GATT, a stipulation exempting member nations from according the most-favored-nation treatment in tariffs and trade, was applied against Japan by most of the countries on grounds of preventing the inflow of cheap Japanese commodities. While the removal of this application is a tribute to Japan's high economic level, discimination in actual practice against Japan—despite the formal amelioration of unequal relations—remains a problem waiting solution.

Concerning the number of export commodities from Japan on which import restrictions continue to be enforced on a wide range, Britain continues to clamp restrictions on 18 items, the three Benelux countries, 38, France, 84, Italy, 116, and West Germany, 28. Notwithstanding the elimination for the most part of Article 35 of GATT in the relations between Japan and the leading nations of Western Europe, the stipulation is enforced not only by Portugal and Spain, but also by some 30 countries, including the developing nations of Africa.

Every effort is being made through GATT and bilateral negotiations for the removal of such discriminations against Japan. Particularly in the case of economically advanced countries, since their attitude is based on the fear that Japanese commodities might seriously disturb their home market, Japan is endeavoring to increase her efforts in an orderly manner, avoiding any sudden substantial increases in export of certain sensitive commodities. However, it is a matter of deep regret that moves to restrict Japanese imports have not subsided in the United States, Canada, Australia, and European countries.

One of the most serious discriminations against Japan

involves the United States import restrictions on cotton textiles. International trade, which figures prominently in the economies of the two countries, has annually been marked by Japan's excess of imports over exports. Although Japan has, at each of the past three meetings of the Japan-United States Joint Trade and Economic Committee, drawn the attention of the United States to the need to correct this anomalous pattern of trade, the latter continues to repeat its assertion that balancing of trade on a bilateral basis is not necessarily imperative if balance is attained on a multilateral basis.

In the case of Japanese exports to the United States, approximately 30 per cent is being subjected to voluntary control, or face the consequences of import control measures.

Likewise, the effects of the stepped up United States policy of "buy American" and "ship American" and its indiscriminate use of the anti-dumping legislation, will no doubt continue to be felt as long as the current policy to protect the dollar is pursued. The solution of these problems will require patience over an extended period.

On the other hand, providing the principle of separating politics from economics is respected, it is the intention of Japan to expand its volume of trade with the communist countries. Although the approval to export a vinylon plant to Communist China, on the basis of a five year extended payment, led to energetic protests from the Chinese Nationalist government, Japan's trading policy with regard to Communist China is based on non-shipment of strategic materials and fixed limitation on the period of long term payments on exports.

chapter 29

Question of Reparations

THE QUESTION of reparations afforded the most crucial test for Japanese diplomacy in the immediate postwar years. In order to fulfill her obligations to the war ravaged countries, as stipulated in Article 14 of the San Francisco peace treaty, Japan intended to pay the reparations in the form of services.

The form which these reparations took in the case of Japan differed in several respects from other types of reparations. For instance, under the Treaty of Versailles at the end of World War I, the victor nations imposed reparations in cash amounting to astronomical figures which vanquished Germany found impossible to pay. This form of reparations not only crippled the German economy and brought on an unprecedented inflation, but it also adversely affected the world economy and the economies of the victor nations themselves.

Firstly, to avoid a similar experience, the amount of reparations imposed on Japan took into consideration not only Japan's ability to pay, but even the pace of her economic recovery. Secondly, the negotiations concerning the amount to be paid and to whom, as well as the period of

173

such payments, were left to Japan and the recipient countries. This form of negotiations ruled out any unilateral imposition of reparations on Japan.

Thirdly, only countries which were occupied by the armed forces of Japan and had sustained losses and damages as a direct result of the Japanese military occupation were eligible to demand reparations from Japan.

Only two countries, the Philippines and Vietnam, demanded and negotiated for reparations from Japan under the provisions of the San Francisco peace treaty. With Burma, which did not participate in the San Francisco peace treaty, and Indonesia, which signed but did not ratify the peace treaty, Japan entered into separate negotiations on reparations. Separate treaties of peace and agreements on reparations were later signed between Japan, on the one hand, and Burma and Indonesia, on the other.

Nationalist China and India signed separate treaties of peace with Japan, but waived all rights to claim any reparations from Japan. Although Cambodia and Laos relinquished their rights to claim compensation, Japan signed economic cooperation agreements with these two nations and offered economic assistance in the form of outright grants. Thus, there were only four countries—Burma, the Philippines, Indonesia, and Vietnam—with whom reparations agreements had to be negotiated.

In principle, Japan's reparation payments were to be in the form of services as specified in the San Francisco peace treaty. In fact, however, Japan assumed the responsibility to pay reparations to Burma, the Philippines, Indonesia, and Vietnam in the form of goods and services with the object of contributing to the recovery as well as active development of the economies of the recipient countries.

Negotiations on reparations with the four countries were conducted over an extended period, during which an interim agreement on the salvaging of sunken ships was also concluded. Every effort was made by Japan to reach an amicable and satisfactory agreement with the countries concerned. Burma was the first to reach a settlement on reparations with Japan. However, in order to cover any eventuality that reparations subsequently agreed to by Japan with the other recipient countries might go beyond what Burma considered to be equitable, she inserted in Article 5 of her peace treaty of 1954, the right to reopen the reparations issue in case such an inequity should arise.

Japan succeeded in concluding reparation agreements with the Philippines in 1956, with Indonesia in 1958, and with Vietnam in 1959. Burma, of course, reopened negotiations on reparations, and a fresh understanding was finally reached after a series of talks. Additional payments were incorporated in the Japan-Burma Economic Cooperation Agreement of March, 1963. With these agreements, Japan has fulfilled her treaty obligations to settle the issue of reparations.

With Laos and Cambodia, which had waived all rights to claim reparations, Japan signed economic cooperation agreements in 1958 and 1959, respectively, offering gratuitous economic assistance. Japan also settled the outstanding issue of the special yen account, debts incurred by Japan during the war, with Thailand in 1955.

Although the payment of reparations is intended to legally compensate the various countries for the material losses and human miseries inflicted in these countries by Japan during the war, the demands made by the claimants were multifarious. All of the claimants being developing countries, Japan's reparations are being paid in the form of an economic cooperation assistance program.

The payment of reparations has enabled Japan to promote reconstruction and developmental activities and contribute to the stability of the people's livelihood in the recipient countries. It has also furnished Japan with an opportunity to introduce its products and technology in Southeast Asia and expand economic exchanges with the recipient nations.

With the exception of Thailand, these countries all regained their independence after the war. They are ardently nationalistic and eager to improve the living standards of their peoples. To achieve their economic goals, they are attempting to make the maximum use of the reparations, the payment of which is an important factor in the friendly ties which Japan maintains with these countries.

In view of the tremendous sums involved in the payment of reparations and the cost of economic cooperation, Japan has had to mobilize her financial resources to fulfill an obligation unprecedented in her history. The total amount involved in reparation payments to Burma, the Philippines, Indonesia, and Vietnam and the gratuitous economic assistance to Laos and Cambodia is ¥366,800,000,000 (approximately $1,020,000,000), of which Japan has as of February 1, 1964, already paid out ¥168,860,000,000 (approximately $470,000,000) or 46 per cent of the grand total.

The sums of reparations involved for the individual countries and the forms of economic cooperation are as follows:

In the case of Burma, the original reparation agreement called for the payment of ¥72,000,000,000 ($200,000,000) over a period of ten years beginning from 1955. As of February 1,1964, Japan had already paid Burma ¥63,800,-000,000 or 88.6 per cent. Major items included ¥10,300,-000,000 for the Balu-Chaung hydroelectric power station; ¥10,500,000,000 for galvanized iron sheets, steel rails, and other metal products; ¥12,100,000,000 for machinery; ¥17,800,000,000 for trucks and other transportation equipment; ¥4,700,000,000 for vehicles, pumps, electrical goods factories, and miscellaneous amounts for canned fish, fertilizer, etc.

The Balu-Chaung hydroelectric plant project was the first of its kind in Burma, and it afforded an opportunity to train Burmese specialists.

As a result of the negotiations reopened by the Burmese government, Burma began receiving after April, 1965 (end of the original reparations obligation) an additional $140,000,000 in the form of economic cooperation over a 12-year period, and $30,000,000 in yen currency as a loan payable in six years.

In the case of the Philippines, the reparations agreement stipulated the payment of ¥198,000,000,000 ($550,000,000) over a period of ten years beginning from July, 1956. As of February 1, 1964, the Philippines had received ¥50,680,-000,000 or 25.6 per cent. The greater part of the payment was in the form of machinery, such as ¥20,300,000,000 for ships; ¥13,400,000,000 for plants; ¥3,500,000,000 for metal products. These goods and services have played an important role in promoting marine transportation and industrialization of the Philippines. Because it is relatively easy for the Philippines to obtain American developmental assistance and relief, the amount of reparation payment still outstanding is comparatively large, being ¥147,300,-000,000.

Moreover, the Philippines concluded an economic cooperation agreement with Japan, simultaneously with the reparations settlement, under which she acquired a yen loan totalling ¥90,000,000,000 payable in 20 years. Out of this sum, $6,527,000 sanctioned in October, 1961, for expanding telecommunication facilities, and $5,220,000 sanctioned in April, 1963, for purchases of materials in connection with the extension of the Cagayan section of the

Manila Railways, have already been paid as part of the reparations.

Furthermore, it was agreed in an exchange of official notes between Japan and the Philippines that the expenditures involved in the construction of the Marikina multi-purpose dam (a section of the Marikina multi-purpose development plan launched in 1957) will also be met as part of the reparations payment. For the construction of this project, the construction firms of the two countries collaborated in the bidding. However, no agreement has been reached on the final sum with the Philippines government. Although surveys have been completed, the main construction work has been held up by the lack of a final agreement and increasing doubts being voiced in the Philippines as to the safety and economic soundness of the project.

In the case of Indonesia, the reparations agreement stipulated the payment of ¥80,300,000,000 ($223,080,000) over a 20-year period commencing April, 1958. As of February 1, 1964, Indonesia had already received approximately ¥40,200,000,000 or 50 per cent. Principal items included ¥7,800,000,000 for ships, ¥8,500,000,000 for plants, ¥8,700,000,000 for various projects, ¥2,300,000,000 for steel rails, and ¥600,000,000 for Koran publication. Among the projects, the Tulungagung diversion tunnel and Hotel Indonesia have already been completed, while the Karangkates dam project and the power plant of the Kalikonto Riam-Kanan Dam are nearing completion. These projects will contribute substantially to Indonesia's developmental plans. Another project is the construction of a 29-story skyscraper, the Wisma Nusantara, in Djakarta.

Under the reparations agreement, Indonesian students and trainees receive specialized training in Japan. A large number of these students have and are still receiving technical education in many fields. Since the training program is bound to have beneficial effects in the future for both Japan and Indonesia, heavy stress is laid on this significant form of rendering services under the reparations agreement. At the same time as the settlement of the reparations issue, Japan signed an economic and development loan agreement with Indonesia, providing $400,000,000 to be payable over a period of 20 years.

In the case of Vietnam, Japan agreed to pay ¥14,040,-000,000 ($39,000,000) over a period of five years beginning January, 1960. As of February 1, 1964, she had already paid ¥12,080,000,000, or 86 per cent. The principal items are ¥9,100,000,000 for the Danhim electric power project, and ¥2,700,000,000 for radios, air conditioners, household electric appliances, paper, dyes, etc.

Construction of the Danhim Dam proceeded so smoothly, since it was launched in April, 1961, that it was completed well ahead of schedule on January 15, 1964. Great festivities attended the completion of the giant project. Having very little coal resources and no oil deposits, South Vietnam must depend on the development of hydroelectricity. Two hydroelectric generators with a total capacity of 45,000 KVA have gone into service, and a further two units are expected to go into operation shortly. When finally completed, the power plant will be one of the biggest in Southeast Asia, providing 160,000 KW of electricity.

Like the other countries receiving reparations, Vietnam also signed a loan agreement with Japan, under which she is to receive $7,500,000 over a three-year period following the coming into force of the agreement. In addition, in an exchange of official documents relating to a separate economic development loan amounting to $9,100,000, loans will be extended on a private basis from the fifth year after the agreement comes into effect. The agreement specifies that the loans will be used for the construction of an urea plant and for the payment of services of necessary Japanese technical personnel and goods.

As for Laos, economic cooperation assistance totalling ¥1,000,000,000 was to have been provided during a two-year period from January, 1959, but successive delays in executing the assistance have caused the program to run into its sixth year. Japan has paid ¥600,000,000 for the Vientiane water works, and ¥260,000,000 for the city's electric power plant. Furthermore, in August, 1962, a loan of ¥425,100,000 was arranged with the Overseas Economic Cooperation Fund to be mainly used for public works.

Economic cooperation assistance to Cambodia amounting to ¥1,500,000,000 was to have been paid within three years, but the period has been extended by two years. This assistance accord has already paid ¥500,000,000 for Pnom Penh's waterworks, ¥300,000,000 for the Tonlesap Bridge, and ¥300,000,000 for agricultural livestock, and a health center.

Lastly, there is the special yen account agreement with Thailand. This debt was incurred by Japan during World War II for the procurement of goods within Thailand and for the provision of Baht currency. Payment was finally made on the balance which remained at the end of the war. The total amounting to ¥9,600,000,000 will be paid in installments over an eight-year period which began in January, 1962.

chapter 30

Assistance to Under-
developed Countries

O N THE PROBLEMS facing the developing nations, Japan is well qualified to express her opinions, having herself experienced such a stage of development. The recovery of the Japanese economy and the German economy in Europe from the ashes of World War II is often described as miraculous, but this high rate of economic development was also experienced in Japan about a century ago during the Meiji Restoration.

During the period of half a century after the latter half of the Meiji Era, Japan's rate of economic growth as a developed nation was higher than the comparative growth registered either in the United States or in the Soviet Union in the forty years after the October Revolution.

With meager capital and scanty resources, Japan has had to rely on mass education, boundless energy, a deep sense of duty, and the courageous spirit of a free people as a generating power to achieve its remarkable economic development. The successful example of Japan can well be a model for the developing nations of the world.

While the industrialized nations of the world have in recent years made considerable progress in stabilizing and developing their economies still further, the developing nations are still unable to provide the vital necessities of life—clothing, food, and housing—for their rapidly increasing populations. The population of the developing nations now totals approximately 1,250,000,000. If the population of China of 600,000,000 is added to this total, they comprise three-fourths of all mankind. Unless the industrialized nations extend effective economic cooperation and assistance to these struggling masses, they will pose a constant threat to the political stability and peace of the world.

During the immediate postwar years, the industrialized nations have had to extend relief to the war devastated nations to assist in the reconstruction of their economies. In their own efforts to maintain a high rate of economic growth, a higher standard of living, and to achieve full employment, a keener realization has been growing among the industrialized nations of the importance of achieving a worldwide economic development and prosperity, particularly among the underdeveloped nations.

It was natural that Japan, devastated by the ruinous war, should have been behind the other advanced nations in giving assistance to the underdeveloped nations. Although private investment overseas was resumed in 1950, it was not until April, 1952, that Japan regained her independence. Initially, the average extent of Japanese capital cooperation was only about $18,000,000 annually. Following the country's participation in the Colombo Plan in October, 1954, the scope of Japan's assistance, mainly technical cooperation, to the developing nations rapidly increased.

Speaking before the National Press Club in Washington, D.C., on November 8, 1954, Prime Minister Yoshida proposed the urgent extension of $4,000,000,000 in economic assistance to the developing countries of Southeast Asia. In his speech, the Japanese Prime Minister Yoshida warned that if the economic development of Communist China should far outstrip the level of development in the neighboring countries of Southeast Asia in the years ahead, this strategic region would fall an easy victim of communism. In order to increase her economic capacity, Communist China was expending huge sums of capital, at least twice the amount per capita of the Southeast Asian countries.

"Unless advanced nations outside the region extend this massive assistance in time," asserted Yoshida, "the free countries of Southeast Asia cannot procure the necessary capital for economic development. Although there are a number of specialized financial agencies supplying capital to the underdeveloped nations of the world, the total of such financial assistance supplied to Southeast Asia amounts to only $400,000,000 annually. This sum was only one-tenth of the capital investment required to compete with the rate of Communist Chinese economic growth. Accordingly, it is necessary to vastly increase the availability of capital on the part of governments and international financial institutions. The people of Japan are prepared to cooperate fully in making the plan successful," assured Yoshida.

Unfortunately, this grandiose program for Southeast Asia did not materialize as Prime Minister Yoshida resigned shortly after delivering the speech. In the light of the prevailing grave circumstances in Southeast Asia, the imperativeness of the program proposed over a decade ago is becoming increasingly apparent.

The main shift in Soviet policy, initiated by Prime Minister Nikita S. Khrushchev after the death of Josef Stalin, advocating reduction and eventual total abolition of armaments, peaceful coexistence and economic competition, has also highlighted the growing importance of economic development.

As part of the United Nations Ten-Year Development Plan, a United Nations Trade and Development Conference lasting nearly three months, was held in Geneva from March 23, 1963. The conference was attended by 121 countries, all members of the United Nations or its specialized agencies (West Germany, Switzerland, Monaco). In addition, observers from GATT, EEC, and COMECON also took part in this mammoth conference of 1,500 delegates. It was an epochal and significant conference in which the entire world discussed methods of dynamically increasing world trade and the problems arising from the North-South relationship.

Prior to the opening of the conference, Chairman Prebisch presented a report outlining the position of the developing nations to be discussed by the conferees. Japan's position vis-a-vis the report may be summarized as follows:

Japan's imports from the developing nations in 1963 totaled $2,620,000,000, or 38.8 per cent of her entire volume of imports. As for exports, the total was $2,550,000,000, or 46.9 per cent of the entire volume of exports, a sizeable balance of trade in favor of the developing nations.

The percentage share of the developing nations in the total exports of the United States in 1962 was only 29 per cent, for countries of the EEC 18 per cent, or a total of only 23 per cent in case of the advanced countries. It is thus apparent that Japan's percentage of exports to the developing nations is incomparably higher than those of the other advanced nations of the West.

With regard to the Prebisch report on higher prices for primary products, since Japan imports a huge volume of primary products, such as wheat, any rise in the price of agricultural products of the temperate zone is a heavy burden on Japan's economy. In 1962, for instance, 74 per cent of the entire imports consisted of primary products, of which half or $2,130,000,000 were imports from the developing countries. Any rise in price will only aggravate the already unfavorable balance of Japanese trade. In concluding commodity agreements, Japan desires that the agreements be limited to only a few tropical products, such as coffee, cocoa, etc.

Concerning preferences for industrial goods, the bulk of manufactured products of the developing countries consists of textiles and miscellaneous goods produced by light industry. By using the system of preferences, such goods could enter Japan and inflict a severe blow on her domestic industry.

Another serious problem which Japan is currently facing is the increasing pressure placed by the United States, and other advanced countries on Japanese products, especially articles produced by the medium and small industries. To protect its interest, Japan will no doubt have to limit the preferences to certain countries, certain commodities, and for a short period of time. In any case, preferences should be applied only to industries which are incapable of meeting competition and should not be applicable to articles which are already threatening Japanese manufactures.

With reference to the question of indemnification, although the IMF has already adopted its principle, the Prebisch report urges the advanced countries to compensate the developing nations for any losses incurred as a result of unfavorable trade. If this system is adopted, the burden on Japan will be intolerable and Japan opposes this suggestion as being impractical.

Despite Japan's earnest desire to do its utmost in the field of assisting the developing nations, it is, of course, not in a position to accept such burdens unconditionally. In certain respects, Japan is still in the intermediate stage of development and must, therefore, adjust the extent of her cooperation and assistance to the developing nations with the marginal profits from her exports and the protective requirement of her domestic industries.

To meet the needs of multi-purpose assistance through international organizations, Japan has already paid in $66,-600,000 to the International Reconstruction and Development Bank (World Bank), $20,700,000 to the International Development Association (Second World Bank) and $2,-800,000 to the International Investment Corporation. To the United Nations Technical Assistance Program she annually subscribes the sum of approximately $2,000,000.

However, most of the economic cooperation projects undertaken by Japan are on a bilateral basis, or 95 per cent of the total, in the form of grants, long-term credits and private investments. One-half of the total sum is in long-term credits, slightly over one-fourth in grants, and one-fourth in private investments. The major part of the grants is under the reparations program or in the form of technical assistance.

Geographically, in 1962, 52.2 per cent of the aid went to Asia, 35.2 per cent to Central and South America, 6 per cent to the Middle and Near East, and the remaining 6.5 per cent to other parts of the world (including contributions to international organizations). In other words, the giant's share of Japanese aid is being directed to Asia and Central and South America. While the aid given to Central and South America is mainly in the form of private initiative, such as private investments and exports credits, nearly two-thirds of the assistance given to Asia consists of reparations or direct loans made in conformance with government policy.

World rivalry between the free world and communist camps, moving from the military sphere of the cold war into the economic sphere, is taking the shape of competition for the economic progress of the developing nations. This intense competition is now being waged over a vast area, from Asia and Africa, to Central and South America.

Under its program of assisting the developing nations, Japan offered a yen loan in the amount of $50,000,000 on a governmental basis to India in 1958. When the consortium of creditor nations to assist India was established in 1958, and one for Pakistan in 1960, Japan did not hesitate to join these organizations. In both quality and volume, Japan rapidly augmented her assistance to the developing nations.

When in March, 1960, the industrially advanced Western nations established the DAG (Development Aid Group) to coordinate aid to the developing nations, Japan also became one of its members. Through these various organizations, Japan's share of capital assistance was $380,000,000 in 1961, fifth among the DAG nations following the United States, France, Britain, and West Germany.

Parallel with the growth in assistance, Japan spared no efforts in endeavoring to improve the type and effectiveness of her aid by improving organizational structures. With this aim in view, she established in March, 1961, the Overseas Economic Cooperation Fund, and in June, 1962, the Overseas Technical Cooperation Corporation. At the same time in October, 1962, when DAG was reorganized as a subsidiary organ of the OECD, Japan continued to be one of the active participants of the newly organized DAC.

In contrast to the problem of East-West relations in the field of assisting the developing nations, the problem of North-South is currently attracting universal interest. The term refers to the mutual relations existing between the industrialized and advanced nations of the Northern Hemisphere, and the agricultural and underdeveloped nations of the Southern Hemisphere. The relationship is further complicated by the cold war rivalry being staged in the developing regions by the non-communist and communist blocs, making the North-South problem inseparable from the East-West problem.

It was against this background that in the spring of 1962, the late President Kennedy proposed a decade of development by the United Nations in the 1960's. In the autumn of the same year, a resolution to this effect was adopted by the 17th United Nations General Assembly. The aim of the resolution was to increase the annual national income of the developing nations by at least five per cent by 1970.

Japan's assistance to developing nations reached its peak in 1961 and has since noticeably declined. In 1961 it stood at $380,000,000, or one per cent of the gross national income, falling sharply in 1962 to $280,000,000, or 0.66 per cent of the national income. A further drop to $270,000,000 was registered in 1963.

The most outstanding fall was seen in long-term export credits. Although more favorable conditions are required to increase trade with the developing nations, Japan is unable to offer the same terms of deferred payment for exports given by West Germany, France, and Britain.

To check the steadily declining pattern of assistance to the developing nations, the Japanese Foreign Office recently formulated a four-point program to increase the volume of aid. The first point was to increase direct government loans by easing the conditions. The second point was to adopt a new system of direct loans, from the multi-nation system sponsored by the World Bank, to a bilateral project loan. The third point was to restore and maintain the volume of assistance to one per cent of the national income. The fourth point was to render technical assistance combined with capital aid in order to enable the developing nations to help themselves.

The new policy of increasing direct government loans included the granting of yen loans not only to India and Pakistan, but to Indonesia, the Philippines, and Taiwan. Efforts to improve the terms of the loans from 5.75 per cent interest payment payable in 15 years, are now being actively considered.

Under the system of project loans, Japan hopes to increase her competitive strength by granting yen loans to certain types of commercial transactions. For example, such loans may be extended to countries which permit Japanese firms to participate in biddings. Loans are cancelled in case Japanese bidders are barred. This system is considered beneficial in promoting the export of Japanese capital goods.

In line with the decision reached earlier by the advanced nations of DAC, Japan is directing her efforts toward expending one per cent of the national income to the assistance program for underdeveloped countries.

For any program of assistance to developing nations to be a success, it is absolutely imperative that the nations receiving aid should have the will and capacity to effectively utilize the aid offered. From this point of view, the advanced nations have recently been stressing the importance of furthering the spirit of self-help and drafting and execution of a well prepared development plan for the underdeveloped countries. In other words, loans are only provided after preliminary surveys and careful studies have been made of the projected enterprise in which technical cooperation is an integral part of that assistance. Under this plan Japan hopes at the same time to promote the export of its products.

Lately, owing to problems of quality and price, as well as domestic pressure by local producers, Japan's imports of primary products from developing nations have increased only very slightly. If the developing nations meet the requirements of Japan on the questions of quality and price, the country is a major promising market for their primary products. Hereafter, it would be mutually beneficial if Japan's economic cooperation and technical assistance can be based on "developmental import," that is to increase the purchases of primary products from developing nations as far as possible.

For Japan, the markets of Southeast Asia are important as outlets for articles produced by her heavy and chemical industries. Japan should shift her exports to heavy industrial and chemical goods from Western Europe to Southeast Asia, at the same time boosting her purchases of raw materials and foodstuffs from the region. By stepping up her technical cooperation, she can at the same time promote greater exports.

Finally, in order to improve her international balance of payments, it is incumbent upon Japan to increase her exports. Serious consideration should be given to the vital role of the construction industry, long overlooked, in enhancing Japanese economic activities overseas.

Although admittedly rather late, the government has lately shown signs of realizing the importance of the engineering industry, such as its move to encourage the merger of the Overseas Construction Cooperation Association and the International Construction Technical Association.

During the postwar years, Western construction firms have remarkably increased their overseas activities, particularly in the developing countries. The various governments have given special consideration to loan interest and tax privileges to facilitate acquisition of foreign bids. When Pakistan announced in 1963 the construction of the world's largest construction project, the Mangla Dam Project costing $350,000,000, several United States firms undertook its construction as a joint venture. Insofar as Asia is concerned, Japan should, for political reasons alone, encourage Japanese construction firms to compete on equal terms with foreign companies, thereby earning much needed foreign exchange and contributing to the improvement of the nation's international balance of payments.

CHAPTER 31

Japan's Fundamental Foreign Policy

THE JAPANESE government and the ruling Liberal-Democratic Party have, under successive cabinets headed by Prime Ministers Kishi Nobusuke, Ikeda Hayato and Sato Eisaku, proclaimed their policy to be based on "Cooperation with the free world community," "support of the United Nations," and "being a staunch member state of the Asian community."

The Constitution of Japan clearly stipulates that Japan is a free and democratic country. We regard this as a golden rule, but in the world of today it is impossible for Japan alone to maintain the system of freedom and democracy.

It is this realization that has given birth to the foreign policy of "cooperation with the free world community." Prime Minister Ikeda has even described Japan as one of the three pillars supporting the free world, the other two being the United States and Western Europe. In essence, this policy stems from the recognition that Japan shares a heavy responsibility in the future development of the free world, both politically and economically.

However, this line of foreign policy, based on the Japan-United States Security Treaty, is mistakenly interpreted by a section of the population as being completely wedded to American policy. However, those who hold such views should thoroughly digest the words of Foreign Secretary Lord Home at the time of the Cuban crisis in the autumn of 1962. He declared that the basic objective of communism of imposing its system on other parts of the world remain unchanged and relentless. We should recognize, he went on, that our security and freedom depend largely on American power and strength. When America is threatened, we are also threatened. America's crisis is our crisis, Lord Home reminded his nation.

Our foreign policy is also based on this precept. The lesson of the Cuban crisis is that world peace and freedom were safeguarded because the United States possessed absolute superiority in military power.

Being a nation fervently dedicated to the principles of peace and freedom, Japan's fundamental foreign policy is aimed at maintaining the system of democracy not only in other parts of the world but in Japan itself. Should this democratic system collapse in other countries on a major scale, it will be impossible for Japan to remain a democratic nation. Accordingly, it is not only natural but an obligation for Japan to cooperate with other democratic nations to preserve their freedom.

From this point of view, it can be readily seen how important is Japan's relations with the United States. On the other hand, the international political influence of the countries of Western Europe, particularly Great Britain and the EEC member states, should not be overlooked. However, during the administration of Prime Minister Kishi, Japan's collaboration with the other free countries was almost entirely confined to the United States.

During the Ikeda administration, ties with Western European countries were forged and strengthened. Between

September and October, 1962, Foreign Minister Ohira Masayoshi visited Western Europe, followed by Prime Minister Ikeda Hayato in November. In return, the Foreign Ministers of Great Britain, France, and Western Germany visited Japan in 1963. Thus, Japan widened the sphere of her diplomatic contacts, which included periodic routine meetings not only with the United States but also with Canada, Britain, France, West Germany, and Australia.

High level personal contacts continued in 1964 when Secretary of State Dean Rusk visited Japan in January, followed in April by French Prime Minister Pompidou accompanied by Foreign Minister Couve de Murville. Visits by other leaders of Western Europe and expected to take place in the near future. By strengthening her ties with the countries of Western Europe, Japan is making a valuable contribution to the unity of the free world.

Having tasted the bitter experiences of the futility of the policy of aggression, Japan has, since the end of the war, devoted herself wholeheartedly to the principles of peace, most eloquently symbolized by her policy of upholding the "spirit of the United Nations." The people of Japan repose the greatest hopes in the United Nations, not only because it relies on the United Nations to guarantee the security of Japan and the peace of the world, but also because of their desire to enhance the nation's international prestige.

With her admission into the United Nations in December, 1956, during the 11th General Assembly session, Japan became an equal partner in the international society of nations. In his speech on the occasion of Japan's admission, Foreign Minister Shigemitsu Mamoru emphasized Japan's determination to fully honor the responsibilities spelled out in the United Nations Charter and her willingness to serve as a bridge of understanding between East and West.

Since the 11th General Assembly of the United Nations,

the world body has been beset by a series of international conflicts, including the problems of Korea, Hungary, Algeria, Cyprus, West Irian, Tibet, Congo, and Cuba. In the solution of these problems, Japan has endeavored to play a mediatory role between the Western nations and the AA group (countries of Asia and Africa), representing the views of the moderate Afro-Asian nations and restraining whenever necessary the radical and so-called non-aligned nations.

Among the numerous problems before the United Nations, Japan has concentrated her efforts on the problem of banning nuclear tests. As the only nation ever to experience the atomic holocaust, Japan's earnest endeavors in this respect were highly evaluated by the other United Nations members. As soon as she entered the United Nations, Japan joined Canada and Norway in proposing a system of giving prior notice of any nuclear test. At the 12th United Nations General Assembly session, Japan submitted her own proposal for the temporary suspension of nuclear tests, a compromise between the Western and Soviet plans. Cooperating with Austria and Sweden at the 13th General Assembly, Japan presented another proposal to ban nuclear testing, and at the 14th General Assembly meeting, became a co-sponsor with other nations of the AA Group to oppose French atomic tests in the Sahara Desert. Japan continued her efforts by voting in favor of a non-nuclear club and the declarations against the use of nuclear weapons at the 16th General Assembly, and in the following year upheld all resolutions that aimed at halting nuclear tests. At the 18th General Assembly, the UN members finally agreed unanimously to ban the launching into space of any nuclear weapon.

On the question of representation of China, Japan, which has consistently supported the position of Nationalist China, is unlikely to change its attitude at the forthcoming session that it regards the issue as an important question requiring a two-thirds majority vote.

In the field of international cooperation by the United Nations, Japan has been active in many spheres. In 1959 she was elected as a governing member of the United Nations Economic and Social Council. Except for the Big Five, Japan's re-election three years later to assume the same post, was unprecedented in ECOSOC history.

Originally the United Nations had 51 members, but has since more than doubled its membership. The question of reorganizing the world body in a more rational manner is receiving wider attention. In this connection, Japan should make every effort to become a permanent member of the United Nations Security Council. In September, 1959, the Conlon Report submitted to the Chairman of the United States Senate Foreign Relations Committee recommended that the United States should, in the event the reorganization of the Security Council comes up for consideration, propose Japan as a permanent member of the Security Council. The report further admits that the Asian nations are inadequately represented on the Council and names Japan and India as fully qualified to assume the responsible post. Public opinion not only in the United States but throughout the world has duly recognized Japan's remarkable economic growth and her international importance, politically and culturally. Japan must be fully prepared to bear the responsibilities of achieving the United Nations goal of world peace.

Japan has two important reasons for adopting the foreign policy plank of acting as a staunch member of the Asian community. The first and most important reason is geographical. Japan desires to have the closest possible political and economic relations with her neighbors and develop neighborly diplomatic ties. Secondly, by cooperating politically and economically with the developing countries of Asia, extending assistance to raise the standard of living and stimulating economic development in the region, Japan will at the same time be able to increase her commercial ties.

Referring to the subject of Japan's future role in the world, former Foreign Minister Okazaki Katsuo said the nation ought to have a grand dream. Urging Japan to endeavor to bring the nations of Asia and Africa closer together, he suggested that Japan's future should be linked to the development and prosperity of the AA region. While I generally agreed with the motivation of this view, I felt that our ties with the countries of Africa were still in the formative stage, that our interests had not yet reached the required level. Rather than disperse our efforts over a wide and relatively unfamiliar region, I emphasized the more urgent necessity of strengthening our present ties with Southeast Asia, reiterating the importance of establishing an Asian-Pacific Collective Organization comprising also the United States, Canada, Australia, and New Zealand. I shall refer to this Asian-Pacific Collective Organization in a separate chapter, but it was highly significant that during his tour of Southeast Asia and Australasia in the autumn of 1963, Prime Minister Ikeda emphasized the need to strengthen the solid ties between Asia and the countries of the Western Pacific.

In conclusion, it is vitally important that Japan's diplomacy should be fully cognizant of the fact that the nations of Asia are intently watching Japan, trying to emulate her remarkable achievements in the economic and other fields. It, therefore, must serve as a guidepost for the free countries of Asia, endeavoring at all times to avoid irrevocable diplomatic blunders on the international scene.

CHAPTER 32

Achievement of
Mutual Security

F OR ANY NATION to exist, much less develop, the assurance of its national security is an indispensable element. While the security of Japan is principally guaranteed by the Japan-United States Mutual Security Treaty, the problem of security in the present-day world is complicated by the monstrously destructive power of nuclear weapons and the sharp divisions between the free and communist worlds.

In the age of nuclear weapons, the attainment of absolute or complete security is no longer a possibility. In commenting on the problem of defense against the hydrogen bomb, the late Sir Winston Churchill solemnly declared that there is no sure defense against weapons of mass annihilation. His words were echoed by the American military analyst Hanson Baldwin, who stated that at present there is no such thing as absolute or complete security. If any nation attempts to seek the impossibility, he cautioned, that nation will destroy itself psychologically and physically.

Under these circumstances, there is nothing Japan can do other than to seek the best possible security. Should she neglect her efforts to acquire the maximum safeguards,

Japan will have forfeited her independence and national security.

Secondly, concerning the problem of building up adequate defensive strength to ensure a nation's security, nations today can no longer depend on independent strength but must rely on collective strength.

The destructive force of nuclear weapons makes it impossible to confine its effects within the borders of a single country. Furthermore, the cost of such weapons makes it prohibitive for any small nation to bear the heavy expenditures.

In the present circumstances, however, the insufficient guarantee of protection offered by the United Nations makes it necessary for nations to rely on bilateral or collective guarantees of security.

By calling upon Japan to adopt neutralism, the Soviet Union and Communist China are not only attempting to drive a wedge between Japan and the United States, but are also conspiring to oust the United States armed forces from Japan. If Japan complied with their demand, it would spell nothing less than national ruin.

Thirdly, the concept of preventing war would entail military preparedness, the possession of massive retaliatory power that would deter the aggressive designs of a potential enemy. An alternative would be the capacity to offer limited resistance, strong enough to make the aggressor think twice before launching an attack. War can be better prevented if these two defensive elements are present. As a rule, however, the big nations have chosen retaliatory power while the small nations have chosen to rely on their power of resistance. Needless to say, the most significant fact about the Japan-United States Security Treaty is its effect in preventing war. In choosing between the security pact with the United States and so-called neutralism, the

primary factor to consider is which of the two contains the
least danger of Japan being embroiled in a nuclear war.

In weighing the awesome possibilities of a limited or all-
out nuclear conflict, it must be said that under the Japan-
United States Security Treaty, the chances of Japan being
drawn into a limited nuclear war are quite remote. Any
nation contemplating an attack against Japan, jointly de-
fended by Japanese and American armed forces, will have
to be prepared to wage either a limited or an all-out war
with the United States.

On the other hand, if Japan becomes neutral, the United
States will lose an important communication, supply and
strategic base in the Far East. Besides, any neutralization
of Japan will also result in the isolation of United States
forces in South Korea, jeopardizing at the same time the
effective defense of Taiwan and the Southeast Asia region.
With the collapse of the United States Far Eastern strategic
setup, the chances of an aggression being launched by the
militarily superior communist forces are admittedly very
large.

As long as the United States maintains a superior military
posture vis-a-vis the forces of the communist world, the
possibility of an all-out nuclear war is almost negligible.
Should such an all-out nuclear war break out, it would
undoubtedly end in the utter destruction of mankind.

In the cold war between the free world and the communist bloc, a factor which has to be considered is the
scheme of the communists to communize the world on the
basis of the dialectical materialism of Marx. Their aim is
to dominate the free countries politically, economically, and
socially. Until they revise their world outlook and adopt a
more flexible attitude, they will never cease their efforts to
subvert the free world in every possible way.

Lately, there have appeared communists who advocate

so-called revisionism, but they are violently denounced by Communist China. The Soviet leadership, which has been fiercely attacked for being revisionists by Communist China, has replied that there can be no peaceful coexistence of ideologies.

Security in the modern world embraces not only the military aspect but political, economic, social, and cultural aspects as well. From the communist outlook, peace is only a continuation of war. The unremitting struggle continues even in times of peace until the entire world is under communist subjugation.

Even Prime Minister Khrushchev has frankly stated that peaceful coexistence is only the continuation of a struggle between two social orders waged in the political, economic, and ideological fields. He has merely confirmed that the struggle continues in all spheres except the military. The real threat to Japan's security today is indirect communist aggression, against which we must always maintain constant vigilance.

Even in the world of today, the ultimate reliance of security lies in the people's realization of national identity, patriotism, and unity. The basis of defending the state has always been and still remains the united will of the people. At the end of the 18th Century, the famous German philosopher, Johann Fichte, declared that in the final analysis the defense of a nation depends not on the excellence of arms nor the number of soldiers, but on the united spirit of the people to resist aggression and defend their country. In whatever age, this eternal truth never changes.

Japan is today an ideal target of communist aggression. Firstly, the roots of freedom have not yet had time to fully mature, and the view of the people toward the sins of communist countries is overly optimistic.

Secondly, there is a wide disparity between the Japanese

and American in their respective views regarding communism. The American people, whose forefathers left 17th Century Europe to seek freedom on the other side of the Atlantic in America and founded the United States after untold hardships, necessarily regard the blessings of freedom in a way that the Japanese would find it hard to imagine. Communist aggression which would destroy individual liberty and human dignity is regarded with deep repugnance. In contrast, the Japanese are generally misled by the artful camouflage of communism and fall easy prey to their honeyed expression of humanitarianism.

Thirdly, there is a strong tendency on the part of the second largest political party, the Socialist Party, in Japan to bandy the world outlook of the communists, not a few of them even going to the extent of assuming the role of Marxists. Some maintain close contact with communist countries and act in such a way with the communists that their identity becomes confusing. A feature of the party which causes grave concern is their so-called people's movement in which the prime object is to obstruct and overturn Japan's security policy.

Should the Socialist Party seize administrative power in the future, there is a strong possibility that the government will not only adopt pro-communist measures, but the entire political structure of the Japanese state will be overhauled in line with communist ideology. The present Japan-United States Security Treaty, valid for ten years, will expire in June, 1970. As long as the Socialist Party continues along the present path Japan may face a grave crisis over the pact's renewal. This possibility has given rise to the oft-quoted phrase: "1970 crisis."

The current situation in the Far East is generally unstable, with the critical areas being Vietnam, Laos, Cambodia and Indonesia. There are many leaders in Japan who do not fully realize the gravity of the situation. It should not be forgotten that the greatest enemy of security is the "sense of false security."

Any serious discussion of Japan's security must involve the problem of revising the Constitution. Since Article 9 of the Constitution prohibits the possession of any war potential, there is a limit to the defensive strength which Japan may maintain. Although the Constitution does not specifically mention the inalienable right of a state to defend itself, Japan's defensive power must still fall short of war potential.

On the question of revising the Constitution, there are both pros and cons. We shall not take up the arguments of those who oppose revision because they are against the Japan-United States Security Treaty. There are those who oppose any revision because they feel the present defensive strength of the country is not unconstitutional. In fact, its legality and constitutionality have already been confirmed by the government, the National Diet, and the Supreme Court. On the other hand, among those who advocate revision, there is a considerable section of opinion which favors a revision of two paragraphs of Article 9, clearly recognizing the legality of the defense forces and their ability to co-operate with the United Nations. They suggest that these two stipulations be adopted in any solution of the problem relating to the defense forces.

In any event, there is little hope that there can be any revision of the Constitution in the foreseeable future. At present the Constitution can be interpreted according to the way the government is handling this delicate problem. Accordingly, it is essential that the government should, regardless of whether it has any intention of revising the Constitution, seriously deal with this problem, clarify its political posture and, at the same time, facilitate the strengthening of the nations's defensive power.

CHAPTER
33

Asian-Pacific Collective Organization

A S MENTIONED earlier, the three pillars of Japan's foreign policy, pursued by the governing Liberal-Democratic Party, have been the upholding of the principles of the United Nations, cooperation with the free nations, and strengthening of its position as a member of the family of Asian nations.

In this connection, I should like to emphasize another aspect of Japan's foreign policy, a vision related to the conception of an Asian-Pacific collective organization. The formation of Pan Asia has long been my advocation, based on the concept of an Asian-Pacific collective organization in which Japan, Southeast Asian countries, Australia, New Zealand, the United States, and Canada would be systematically organized, politically, economically, and culturally.

As the world is getting increasingly smaller, owing to the amazing development of science and technology, the materialization of the vision for regional collective organizations throughout the world is being vigorously advocated by hitherto unassociated independent states.

Prime Minister Ikeda, in a speech on his administrative policies in January, 1964, declared: "I believe that it would

203

be of vital importance for the stability and prosperity of Asia to cultivate and strengthen the groundwork of solidarity among the countries of Asia and the adjacent Western Pacific."

Hitherto, the Japanese government and the Liberal-Democratic Party have not gone beyond economic and technical cooperation in promoting any systematic organization in the Asian-Western Pacific region, but unless closer political links can be forged with these countries, the development of economic ties will be limited.

In Europe, three international organizations have already come into existence, beginning with the ECSC (European Coal and Steel Community), EEC (European Economic Community) and EURATOM (European Community of Atomic Energy). With growing signs of economic integration among the European countries, a new conception of political unification, aiming at the establishment of a European collective organization, is gaining momentum. Walter Hallstein, Chairman of EEC, has categorically stated that any attempt to settle the future question of a collective European organization by separating economic integration from political unification is doomed to failure.

Whether the European collective organization takes the form of a United States of Europe, as advocated by Konrad Adenauer, former Chancellor of West Germany, and Paul-Henri Spaak, Belgian Foreign Minister, or is conceived as a federation of sovereign states, as favored by President de Gaulle, is still open to debate.

On the other hand, while Britain eventually is expected to become a member of ECC, the basis for the formation of an Atlantic Community, including the United States and Canada, has already been agreed upon in the NATO Council. In preparation for the advent of this new Atlantic Community, the United States has been extending loans to the ECSC, cooperating with EURATON on atomic energy, and has legislated the Trade Expansion Act.

The fear that the so-called Kennedy Round of talks, aimed at general reduction of GATT tariffs on trade, would be suspended as a result of the sudden and tragic death of President Kennedy, has now been dispelled by his successor, President Johnson, who has reaffirmed that he would continue the Kennedy policy.

Support for the conception of an Asian-Pacific collective organization, similar to the European-Atlantic Community, has been steadily growing in Asia in recent years. One evident sign of this tendency was seen at the three-power summit meeting in Manila, attended by the leaders of Malaya, the Philippines, and Indonesia in August, 1963, at which an agreement was initiated to unite for the first time in history 150,000,000 people of Malay origin in a single federation called Maphilindo. In September, the new state of Malaysia was proclaimed, uniting the former states of Malaya, Singapore, Sarawak, and Sabah (North Borneo) under a federal government.

An armed conflict, however, broke out between Indonesia and Malaysia. In face of the serious Indonesian guerrilla attacks against Sarawak and Sabah, Malaysia sought and received British military assistance. Japan, for her part, promptly offered her good offices to mediate. A temporary cease-fire was achieved on January 27, 1964, and in February the Foreign Ministers of Malaysia, Philippines, and Indonesia met in Bangkok to try to resolve the dispute on a more permanent basis. It is hoped that the three countries will revive the Maphilindo concept and work toward the achievement of stability in the Southeast Asian area.

In the autumn of 1963, when Prime Minister Ikeda visited the regions of Southeast Asia and the Western Pacific, the purpose of his tour was not merely confined to good-will and the solution of pending problems between Japan and the countries of this important area, but to explore the possibilities of taking a positive step in the direction of organizing and uniting the countries of Asia.

Moreover, Japan has associated herself with the OECD (Organization for Economic Cooperation and Development) a collective organization of the world's industrially developed nations. By her membership in the organization, Japan has assumed heavy responsibilities to cooperate in sustaining the free world as one of the three main pillars along with the United States and Europe.

Greatly inspired and encouraged as a youth by the ideals of Pan Europe of Count Coudenhove-Kalergi of Austria in the years after World War I, I lent myself whole-heartedly to the Pan Asia movement. The ideals of Pan Europe appealed also to such leading French statesmen as Herriot and Briand, as well as other democratic leaders and economists of countries which extolled the principles of democracy.

In the spirit of a great European statesman, French Prime Minister Herriot told the National Assembly: "My fondest hope is to see one day the establishment of the United States of Europe." In the preface of my book, "Pan European Movement and Pan Asian Movement," I para-phrased the words of Herriot and declared that "My greatest hope is to see one day the establishment of a federation of Asia." The ideal, as envisaged at the time, was to create a region of peace in Asia within the framework of the League of Nations.

The ideal of European unity suffered a serious setback with the rise of Nazism in Germany, but it rose like a phoenix out of the ashes of World War II. Whether it is Pan Europe or Pan Asia, I believe that the formation of such a regional collective organization is the dictate of history.

It is a fallacy to consider that the concept of Asian federation is motivated by anti-communism. I entirely agree with the statement of the late President Kennedy that the isolation of the people on the China mainland with the peoples of the Pacific region is a great world tragedy of our times, and it is desirable that this state of affairs should be only a passing phenomenon.

APPENDIX
Chronological Treaty Highlights

1854 Treaty of Kanagawa (Japan-U.S. Treaty of Friendship) *first treaty to be concluded with Western power*

1855 Japan-Russian Treaty of Friendship *defines territorial limits of both countries*

1857 Treaty of Shimoda (Japan-U.S.)

1858 Japan-U.S. Treaty of Amity and Commerce (Treaty of Ansei) *opens new ports*

1885 Tientsin Covenant (Japan-China) *permits both countries to send troops into Korea*

1894 Anglo-Japanese Treaty of Commerce and Navigation *first treaty based on equality*

1895 Treaty of Shimonoseki (Japan-China Peace Treaty)

1902 First Anglo-Japanese Alliance

1904 Japanese-Korean Protocol *empowers Japan to take protective military measures in Korea*

1905 Katsura-Roosevelt Understanding

1905 Portsmouth Treaty (Russo-Japanese Peace Treaty)

1905 Second Anglo-Japanese Alliance *offensive and defensive; recognizes Japan's paramount interests in Korea*

1905 Second Japanese-Korean Protocol *gives Japan virtual control over Korean foreign affairs*

1905 Treaty of Peking (Japan-China) *China transfers Russian holdings to Japan*

1907 Franco-Japanese Agreement

1907 Motono-Iswalsky Agreement (Russia-Japan) *secret clauses*

1907 Third Japanese-Korean Agreement *gives Japan control over Korea's internal affairs*

1908 Root-Takahira Agreement (Japan-U.S.) *reaffirms "open door" principles*

1909 Knox Neutralization Plan for Manchurian Railways

1910 Second Motono-Iswalsky Agreement (Japan-Russia) *mutual assistance pact*

1910 Treaty of Annexation (Japan-Korea)

1911 Second Anglo-Japanese Treaty of Commerce and Navigation *Japan gains customs autonomy*

1911 Third Anglo-Japanese Alliance *third-party arbitration clause*

1912 Third Russo-Japanese Agreement *divides Inner Mongolia into east and west spheres of influence*

1914 London Declaration *signatories promise not to engage in secret peace talks*

1915 Twenty-One Demands (Japan-China)

1916 Fourth Russo-Japanese Agreement *divides all of China; mutual assistance against trespassers*

1919 Versailles Peace Treaty *ends WWI; Japan gets German Far East holdings north of equator*

1921 Four Power Treaty (Japan, U.S., Great Britain, France) *maintains Far East status quo*

1922 Naval Limitation Treaty (Japan, U.S., Great Britain, France, Italy)

1922 Nine Power Treaty (Japan, U.S., Great Britain, France, China, Italy, Belgium, Netherlands, Portugal) *defines open door and equal opporunity*

1940 Tripartite Treaty (Japan, Germany, Italy)

1941 Russo-Japanese Neutrality Pact

1951 Treaty of Peace (Japan and 48 nations)

1951 Japan-U.S. Mutual Security Treaty

1952 Sino-Japanese Peace Treaty (Nationalist China)

1952 Japan-India Peace Treaty

1954 Japan-Union of Burma Peace Treaty

1954 Japan-Union of Burma Reparations and Economic Cooperation Agreement

1956 Japan-Soviet Union Joint Declaration *terminates WWII, restores diplomatic relations*

1960 Revised Japan-U.S. Security Treaty *more favorable to Japan; adds economic clause*

1962 Anglo-Japanese Treaty of Commerce and Navigation

1963 Japan-Burma Economic Cooperation Agreement

1963 Franco-Japanese Commercial Agreement

Index

Indonesia, 174–176, 178–179, 201, 205

International Development Association, 186; *see also* Second World Bank

International Investment Corporation, 186

International Monetary Fund(IMF), 168–169, 185

International Reconstruction and Development Bank, 186, 188, *see also* World Bank

Iswalsky, 48, 50

Ito, Hirobumi, 27, 31–32, 42

Iwakura, Tomomi, 20

Iwo Jima Island, 121

Japan, Burma Economic Cooperation Agreement, 175; *see also* Burma; Constitution, 202; Defense Agency, 99; economic diplomacy, 167–168, 170; Korean annexation, 59; Liberal Democratic party, 86, 100–101, 164, 191, 203–204; National Police Reserve, 98; occupation of, 81, 83–85, 89, 93, 116; reparations, 87–88, 129, 132, 148–149, 153, 168, 173–180, 186; Safety Agency, 98–99; Socialist party, 100, 125, 201; Soviet Joint Declaration, 109, 112; U.S. Joint Trade and Economic Committee, 172; U.S. Mutual Security Treaty, 89–91, 98–99, 191, 197–199, 201–202, revision of, 97–100, 103, revised, 104, 107, 109, 138, 146; U.S. Treaty of Amity and Commerce, 17; U.S. Treaty of Friendship, 16

Japanese immigration, 42, 45, 61

Japanese-Korean Protocol, 57; second, 58

jo-i, 14

Johnson, Lyndon B., 158, 205

Kaiser Wilhelm II, 26

Kajima, Morinosuke, 144–147; *see also* Preface

Kanagawa, 15; Treaty of, 16

Kato, Takaaki, 28, 32, 66–68

Katsura, Premier, 43–44

Katsura-Harriman provisional memorandum, 43–44

Katsura-Roosevelt Understanding, 58

Kennedy, John F., 117–119, 158, 188, 205, 207

Khrushchev, Nikita, 105, 113, 167–168, 183, 200

Kimberly, Lord, 23, 28

Kimil Sung, 125

Kishi, Nobusuke, 99–100, 104–105, 117, 162, 191–192

Knox Neutralization Plan for Manchurian Railways, 44–45, 49, 50, 74

Knox, Philander, 44

Komura, Baron, 43–45

Kondo, Shigezo, 14

Korea, 32, 73, 194; annexation by Japan, 59; independence from China, 26, 30; independence from Japan, 110; in Sino-Japanese War, 32; Japan relations, normalization of, 123–136; Japanese interests in, 39, 45, 54, 57–58, 62; North, 84, 124–125, 133; Republic of, 85, 124–127, 129–130, 132–133, 135–136; Russian influence expelled, 40; Russian penetration of, 31, 33; South, 85, 123–126, 128

Korean People's Democratic Republic, *see* Korea: North

Korean War, 85, 94, 97–98, 104, 125, 132, 137, 152, 155